RECLAIM THAT

First published in 2015 by New Holland Publishers Pty Ltd
London • Sydney • Auckland

The Chandlery Unit 704, 50 Westminster Bridge Road,
London SE1 7QY, United Kingdom
1/66 Gibbes Street, Chatswood, NSW 2067, Australia
5/39 Woodside Ave, Northcote, Auckland 0627, New Zealand

www.newhollandpublishers.com

A record of this book is held at the British Library and the
National Library of Australia.

ISBN 978 1 74257 799 9

Managing Director: Fiona Schultz
Publisher: Christine Thomson
Project Editor: Anna Brett
Design: Lorena Susak and Thomas Casey
Production Director: Olga Dementiev
Printer: Toppan Leefung Printing Limited

10 9 8 7 6 5 4 3 2 1

Keep up with New Holland Publishers on Facebook
www.facebook.com/NewHollandPublishers

RECLAIM THAT

Upcycling your home with style

Words and photography by **Sarah Heeringa**

Additional photography by **Jane Ussher** and **Tony Brownjohn**

NEW HOLLAND

To my dear mother Marion, late grandma Muriel and friend Elizabeth (Ibby) who have all inspired and nurtured me over the years with their creative homemaking.

Contents

Introduction

Introduction

Where does the instinct to make a home come from? In the earliest societies, people decorated their huts with wall paintings and pottery and created comfortable corners to rest in using animal skins. This inclination to gather objects together to furnish the place we call home is basic human behavior, shared by many cultures over many generations. Whether we live in a tiny apartment or large family dwelling, our aspirations often seem the same; typically we want our homes to be a welcoming, inspirational and nurturing space for those who live or stay with us. To this end we fill our houses with tables, chairs, mirrors and other practical things we consider necessary to function. We add comfort, warmth and color with layers of fabric and soft textures. And then there are all the other less obviously useful objects we accumulate because they have sentimental or other value, which we like to have about us. Sometimes the balance tips to where we have so many things in our homes that the sheer amount of stuff feels overwhelming, even to the point of getting in the way of everyday living. But generally speaking, we try to keep our possessions in some sort of order, and hope that others might appreciate our embellishments as an expression of our personal style, home management skills or good taste.

Today, we live in a throwaway society. This is an age of material abundance and as consumers we have more shopping options available to us than any generation before us. Shopping is a popular pastime for many – and if we fancy a particular item for our home, or are simply tired of our how things look and want to switch them for something else, we usually can. When things break or go out of fashion, it is a relatively easy matter to toss that object away and replace it with something shiny and new. At its most extreme, materialism can lead us to believe that happiness and emotional satisfaction can be found in the accumulation of things.

Reclamation offers an antidote to unsatisfying materialism. Through the rediscovery, repurposing and reusing of previously unwanted objects we can achieve some of our home furnishing goals, and in the process, become more aware of our relationship with material things.

The freedom we enjoy to choose what we surround ourselves with is a relatively new cultural phenomenon. In the 18th century and earlier, most people's households were equipped with the very basic objects of everyday life. The grand homes of the genteel classes might have been decorated with elaborate fabrics and exotic furnishings, but most folk had to get by with what

household items had been passed down to them by previous generations, what was made or sold locally or what they managed to cobble together themselves.

Everything was handmade and labor intensive. The fabric used to make clothes and soft furnishings, for instance, took countless hours to be spun and woven before finally being cut and sewn into shape. The historian Eve Fisher has estimated it would have taken 500 hours of hand labor just to create one shirt (*Stuffocation*, 2014).

The industrialization of the 19th century introduced mass production. As prosperity grew, people began to desire the trappings of wealth to reflect their new status.

The term 'Interior Decorator' was first used in America in the early 1900s, and in 1913, New York socialite and interior designer Elsie de Wolfe put her name to the interior design book, *The House in Good Taste*.

By the mid- to late-19th century, interior design had become a thriving industry in industrial countries, and as their economies have grown in the decades since, home furnishings have become available at ever-cheaper prices. The post-war manufacturing boom that lasted until the early 1970s coincided with the baby boom and the rise of suburbia. These mega trends spurred on the mass production of home building and furnishing materials including laminates and synthetic

fabrics. Nowadays, thanks to globalization, low-wage factories in far-away places can mass-produce seemingly limitless numbers of cheap consumer goods, making it more possible than ever to fill our homes with new things at a relatively low cost. Meanwhile the widespread popularity of interior decorating and design as a recreational pastime has grown even more ubiquitous from the late 1990s onwards with the advent of hugely successful home renovation reality television shows.

Here's a question to consider; now we can choose to fill our homes with pretty much anything we like – what do we most want?

Today's home decorator can choose any interior design style from baroque, art nouveau or art deco, to a French country or rustic bohemian look, or the clean lines of post modernism. Or we might opt for eclecticism, juxtaposing elements of them all. So now that we have more homeware and decorating options available to us than ever before, why would we choose to fill our houses with the same shop-bought items as everyone else. After all, surely the best forms of interior decorating are more than simply mimicking a style or ripping out what was there before and replacing it with something new. It's about creating domestic spaces that feel good to be in, that convey a sense of belonging for the people who live there. It's about having the confidence to surround ourselves with things that express our personal style, that have meaning for us or that tell a story. And it is the addition of these subtle and genuine touches that help make a house a home.

Reclaimism is the art of giving old products new value. It offers shopping lovers the thrill of the chase – rummaging through markets and hunting online or through second hand stores for that quirky collectable or unexpected discovery. It's about learning to recognize quality materials and the evidence of skilled workmanship. It embraces upcycling, and the use of our imagination in the process of fixing things up and personalising objects to our own liking. The reclamation approach gives expression to our creativity and delivers more satisfaction than simply buying something can ever generate.

Reclamation is a means of escaping the cycle of buying cheaply made and mass-produced. Instead it can help us to live by the principle of 'buy once, buy well'. Reclamation can be an extremely cost-effective way to furnish our homes, and with the money saved, over time we can add to our upcycled pieces with other quality items made with skill by craftspeople and artisans.

In the throwaway culture in which we live, reclamation offers us more resourceful, more cost effective and more planet-friendly ways to surround ourselves with things we love. It can enrich our lives by helping us celebrate and enjoy objects that tell a story or have meaning and value for us. It's a means by which we can discover and develop new skills. Most importantly, reclamation is about starting at whatever stage we are at now – building on whatever basic abilities and resources we have to begin with.

The Life Cycle of Everyday Things

The Life Cycle of Everyday Things

When you hold onto an everyday item for long enough it sometimes becomes imbued with a greater significance than you might ever have imagined. Here is a short story about such a piece of furniture.

I was about four months pregnant with my first child and returning home from work one day when my husband Vincent surprised me with the delivery of the generously proportioned 1940s lounge suite – in faded, but original, floral brown velvet.

We'd happened, the previous weekend, to walk past the curvaceous suite sitting outside a local second-hand shop and I had remarked, 'Now that's a great sofa'. Our house at the time was very sparsely furnished – decorated with random bits and pieces picked up during our university student days combined with what we had been given as wedding presents. We were living on the tightest budget and things were likely to get even leaner once the baby arrived. However Vincent had decided to seize the moment – and the lounge suite. Unbeknown to me, he had returned later in the week to the second hand store and made the purchase.

As a genuine vintage item, the sofa wasn't cheap to buy. When it was first delivered home, its springs were already starting to soften and sag and the brown and once-gold piping was coming loose. In one or two places, the scratchy coir fibre was even starting to peek through. But we didn't care. It was a fabulously rumpty old suite – with chairs deep enough to sink into, armrests wide enough to comfortably balance a book or a mug of cocoa on, and an elongated sofa frame long enough to allow you to stretch out and fall asleep.

When someone hangs around the family for a long time and their presence gets so familiar that we hardly notice them, we say they've become part of the furniture. But what do you say about your rumpty old sofa that's been around for just as long?

The intention was always to have the whole suite recovered, but somehow we never quite had the spare cash for the job. In the meantime, a whole lot of everyday living happened around the couch and its matching pair of old chairs. Babies were breastfed and toddlers cuddled, art house movies were watched and Saturday night sports games won and lost. When we threw parties and chairs were in short supply, friends perched happily on the suite's generous arms.

At times the sofa doubled as a pirate ship for rambunctious boys, and later – after a baby girl arrived in the house – the sofa was alternately a doll's hospital or a shop. Meanwhile a succession of small children helped bounce the sofa's metal springs into total surrender and fed jammy toast and small plastic toys into the sofa's mysterious cobwebby depths.

At one stage I bought a large bolt of navy blue material from an outlet store and made loose covers, secured at the sides with fabric knots. A few years later I laboriously measured, cut and sewed fitted fabric covers – this time in indigo blue. More years and several house moves later, the sofa and chairs were looking decidedly worse for wear. We sent the suite away, bouncing on the back of a trailer, for a five-year sojourn at a beach house we shared with friends. After several years guests who stayed at the beach house began to complain about the saggy state of the sofa and we began to suspect that small critters might have found a welcoming home in is its rusty interior.

When someone hangs around the family for a long time and their presence gets so familiar that we hardly notice them, we say they've become part of the furniture. But what do you say about your rumpty old sofa that's been around for just as long?

By the time the suite was lugged and bumped on the long journey back into town, the intention to recover had become a decision of do or die. The suite's old wooden frame was still sound, but the springs had completely gone and the dusty coir stuffing mostly needed to be replaced. We either had to find the cash for a complete rebuild – which was now a significant investment – or consign the suite to the dump. As we counted our pennies and contemplated the various fabric, foam and piping options, the sofa sunk to its lowest point of existence. In the intervening months it was left to rest on our wooden veranda and the sofa was claimed by the family Labrador as a grand doggie bed. After so many indignities, the moment for a glorious reinvention of the sofa appeared to have finally arrived.

Now already several years on from it's transformation, it is not inconceivable to imagine I might be sipping cups of tea on this same sofa well into my dotage.

Your
Creative
Eye

Entering a second hand store stocked with a gallimaufry of things can sometimes be a little overwhelming. But what looks like a confused jumble of objects to some, is a treasure trove of opportunity for the bargain hunter and the experienced collector.

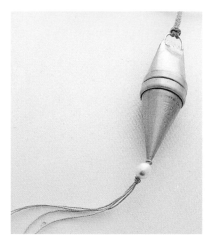

Your Creative Eye

In the course of my work on magazines I am fortunate to have met many creative people who have made upcycling their everyday business. These clever folk reclaim various materials to create useful, well-designed and often delicately beautiful things.

For example one young entrepreneur set up a successful shoe-making factory using salvaged rubber, canvas and other industrial materials, sourced from local companies. The shoes were popular; they were cleverly designed and well made.

Another inspirational artisan was a craft jeweller who had chosen to work with silver and found objects. The day I visited her studio she was creating brooches using small pieces of woolen blanket, and the metals from old silver spoons and pieces of rustic kitchen graters, pictured opposite. Between her skilled fingers she also crafted vintage pearl beads and small metal piping nozzles from retro icing sets into the most delicate pendant necklaces.

In the same month, while researching magazine stories, I came across a group of university spatial design students who had used discarded electric cable wire to create a range of stylish modern furniture. They first plated the colorful plastic-coated wires together, then wove and stitched the wire fabric onto reconstructed frames made from old school chairs and upcycled pallet wood.

From where does this kind of ingenuity spring? It starts with being open to possibilities and looking at everyday objects in a new way – in particular the materials typically consigned to second hand shops or otherwise destined for the rubbish dump.

We may not share the same level of artisan skill, but we all have the option of looking more closely at the objects that are around us and considering if we might use those things in another way. Take, for example, the old wooden tool files in the photo top left. When I bought them second hand they were scruffy and grubby, having come straight from a mechanic's garage. After a scrub with hot soapy water and a new coat of paint, one file box became a useful holder of art supplies (see overleaf) and the other was used for storing sewing miscellany (see page 146).

The difference between seeing something as rubbish or as a potentially valuable resource is in the eye of the beholder. Entering a second hand store stocked with a gallimaufry of things can be overwhelming. But what looks like a confused jumble of objects to some, is a treasure trove of opportunity for the bargain hunter and the experienced collector. The ability to see things afresh is a skill that can be learned and practiced.

It helps if we can embrace the idea of beauty in imperfection. As the Japanese art and philosophy *Wabi-sabi* suggests, there is authenticity and profundity to be found in flawed, rough and natural objects. Things that are old, and that show the wear and tear of time, have more value rather than less. Because reclamation involves playing around with otherwise unwanted things, it can be very liberating. We can allow ourselves the freedom to take risks and experiment. It doesn't matter a jot if we make mistakes. And in the process we can feel our confidence, and our ability to be inventive, steadily grow.

The best way to embark on any creative project is simply to begin – and where better than with choosing an old picture frame, piece of furniture or other simple object that you would like to reclaim.

You can find objects to upcycle in many places. Charity shops, antique fairs, garage sales, school fundraiser carnivals and car boot sales offer a vast array of treasures and trinkets. If you are open to opportunity, a surprising number of great items can also be found for free. Where I live, people will occasionally put old furniture, doors and other miscellaneous items onto the grass verge outside their houses. Many cities also have designated days where unwanted inorganic material can be put out on the curb for the rubbish collectors to pick up. That is if no one takes it away first. I have acquired many things this way, including plush rugs, antique picture frames, retro tables, Italian-made light fittings and enough chunky wooden outdoor chairs to make several matching sets.

If picking things off the side of the road puts you beyond your comfort zone, second hand retail stores, online stores and trading websites are all great places to find goods at very reasonable prices.

Antique and newer second hand items – including things you might get for free – are often far better made, using higher quality materials and with greater workmanship, than their brand new equivalents. For instance, the older the furniture, the more likely it is to be made with oak, kauri, mahogany, or other quality hardwoods. An extreme example of this are Chippendale chairs, made with a species of mahogany called Swietenia mahogany, considered to be the very best wood for delicate woodwork, and chair making in particular, but which is now extremely rare due to over-harvesting.

Take a close look at your object; consider what it is made of, what its best features are and how you might improve or enhance it. Could it be transformed, with a bit of creativity, into something stylish and useful? Practice the habit of looking at objects in a new light, considering how else you might use them. Could that small filing cabinet be used as a bedside cabinet, or that bookcase be mounted on the wall as a set of shelves? Imagine what that piece of wooden furniture might look like if it was whitewashed or painted in a bright color. What might that fabric covered chair look like if it was recovered in florals or a bold stripe?

William Morris, the English textile designer, poet and activist once said; 'If you want a golden rule that will fit everything, this is it: Have nothing in your houses that you do not know to be useful or believe to be beautiful.' This maxim has been repeated often enough to become a cliché – but that doesn't stop it from being a helpful guiding principle. There is a simple pleasure to be had from using even the most humble everyday items when they are both beautiful and useful.

The reclaimer can take Morris' principle a step further. Ask yourself if the object in question can be mended, made beautiful, or otherwise put to good use. Learn to look past the tatty state or boring appearance of an item, to recognize the object's potential and to consider how you might breathe new life into it.

William Morris once said; 'If you want a golden rule that will fit everything, this is it: Have nothing in your houses that you do not know to be useful or believe to be beautiful.' The reclaimer can take this principle one step further. Ask yourself if the object in question can be mended, made beautiful or otherwise put to good use.

Think about the furnishings you already own. Unless we are moving country most of us don't start with a blank canvas when we decorate our homes. We typically bring with us a few things we have bought or acquired as students, things passed down from other family members, wedding presents or other gifts we may or may not particularly like, and other knick knacks we have picked up along the way, which may have more sentimental than aesthetic value.

Can this new piece compliment what you have, or a future look you are trying to achieve? If collecting comes easily to you, at this point you might need to be a little ruthless. When it comes to matter of design, more is often not more. Like a stylish outfit that you put together, you need to visualize the look you are going for and remain consistent. What you don't want to replicate at home is the chaotic melee of the jumble sale table.

Give yourself time to mull over a project and allow inspiration to come to you. Often the best ideas take time and more than one attempt. The French polymath and pioneering mathematician Henri Poincaré captured it perfectly when he wrote the following, 'Often when one works at a hard question, nothing good is accomplished at the first attack. Then one takes a rest, longer or shorter, and sits down anew to the work. During the first half-hour, as before, nothing is found, and then all of a sudden the decisive idea presents itself to the mind. It might be said that the conscious work has been more fruitful because it has been interrupted and the rest has given back to the mind its force and freshness.'

It might take more money than talent to visit an interiors store and kit out a room with a range of coordinated mass-produced homewares. The easiest decorating option is often to buy cheap items created in modern sweatshops at great cost to the environment. But what is the quality or authenticity of such things and why would you want to fill your home with them? How satisfying to instead furnish your home with objects that have stories and a sense of connection, including items that have been saved from being abandoned or dumped in a landfill.

The real skill is in taking old and new, precious and functional, and melding these disparate objects together into a look that is cohesive, pleasing – and personal to you. It requires knowing what to add – and what to reinvent or let go. The result can be the difference between walking into a room that looks like a show home yet lacks character, and a home that exudes warmth, unique style and personality.

Getting
Started

Getting Started

Congratulations, you have made the decision to express your creative spark through upcycling. So what are the next steps? As mentioned in the previous chapter, the best way to embark on any creative project is simply to begin. Once you have found a piece of furniture, antique picture frame or some broken item to upcycle, the next step is to collect the necessary tools and equipment for the project at hand, and set up a suitable area to work.

You can allow yourself permission to make a mess – and to make a few mistakes. A little chaos is an important part of the creative process. However, as much as you may be inspired by your newfound passion for upcycling, it is unlikely that everything else in your life can suddenly be put on hold. Unless you are a free agent of independent means, there are a few practical considerations to work out in order to accommodate other demands on your time and space.

It is frustrating to drag out paints and other supplies in order to embark on a project, only to have to put everything away again a short time later. A preferred scenario – which may, or may not be achievable – is to have the space to lay out the current project you are working on, returning to it later as time permits. Depending on the size and nature of each project you are working on, you may at times also need access to an outdoor or garage area for sanding and a clean and well-ventilated space in which to paint and leave things to dry.

As you begin, consider how you might make the most of whatever space is available to you, and minimize the impact on others, by setting up an area in a garage, basement, hallway, or spare corner of a room. See Space to Create, page 86, for more suggestions about how to achieve this. Wherever you set up your workspace, aim to keep your tools and working materials arranged as compactly and logically as possible.

Several frequently quoted psychological studies suggest that messy work spaces are associated with higher levels of creativity and the generation of new ideas. That may be true, but the effect of a messy space can also be depressing and sap your energy. If you are working on a practical project you don't want to be tripping over paint pots and other materials, nor do you want to waste time looking for that screwdriver or roll of tape you know you have somewhere but cannot find.

Paint boxes all one color
for a uniform look and to
reduce visual clutter. I use
black card and a white
pencil to add labels to
the front of the boxes.

Sewing
ribbons
zips
curtain cord

Photo archive

Papers to action!

FILING

MAPS

Without getting too preoccupied with a need for order, work out an organizational style that inspires you to get started and where handy resources are close at hand.

Find an old wooden hutch dresser or large bookshelf that provides storage with drawers or shelves, as well as a sturdy top for stacking larger items and extra containers. See page 174 for details on how the dresser (left) was reclaimed. Alternatively look for a manrobe, wardrobe, armoire or other form of movable cupboard with doors. You may need to retrofit existing shelves to suit your needs. A lockable wardrobe can be a great solution when space is limited and small children in the house necessitate shutting everything away. Use an outsized art folder to store large papers, sheets of glass or other flat materials and slide it behind the bookshelves or cabinet when not in use.

An advantage of open shelving is that you can easily see and access your materials, but they can quickly look messy and cluttered. Use baskets or sturdy boxes on the shelves in which to cluster supplies. Paint the boxes all one color for a uniform look and to reduce visual clutter. I use black card and a white pencil to add labels to the front of the boxes.

Recycled glass jars can be used for sorting and storing nails, screws, old buttons, small tubes of glue, handy bits of wire and so on. You will likely have an endless supply of lidded jars coming from your kitchen. Simply wash the jars and soak off labels so they are ready to use. Jars in all sizes, enable you to have a place for multifarious small craft items, making them easy to locate when you want them. Collected together, shiny glass jars look very pleasing and once this system is established it is relatively easy to maintain. You can paint the jar lids to make an assortment look like a matching set. See page 184 for a step-by-step guide.

For extra storage use a wheeled cabinet you can roll out when required, or a large lidded container on wheels that you can tidy away in a cupboard or closet. Second hand wooden kitchen trolleys and repurposed small office filing cabinets are great options. Not only are they more sturdy than their modern plastic counterparts, they are far more attractive. If you find a non-wheeled cabinet that suits your needs, it is an easy matter to attach a set of castor wheels. Hardware stores stock castor wheels in a variety of sizes, which can be simply screwed into place. If the cabinet it made of metal you will need to drill holes first using an electric drill and a narrow drill bit. Check the size of the wheels will be adequate for the weight of the cabinet and its contents.

If more storage is required consider hanging baskets from the ceiling above your cabinet – but only do this if it can be achieved without making the space look overly cluttered and crowded.

Allow yourself space to store useful tools such as hammers, a staple gun, a craft knife, pliers, screwdrivers, paintbrushes and a range of sandpapers. My favorite screwdriver is the square headed screwdriver, as unlike older style screws, the tip of the tool does not slip out and burr the screw head easily. Use a pegboard, tool box or series of shallow trays to store your small handtools.

Think about places to store items you plan to reclaim. Resist the temptation to simply hoard large numbers of things – such as endless craft materials or items to be upcycled. There is no limit to the number of possible reclamation projects or materials that can be saved from being put in the bin, so you need to be realistic about how many projects you can complete over a given period.

Aim to complete one project at a time and endeavor to put each finished item to use before starting another. If you have no use or space for the item you have reclaimed, give it to family and friends or sell it online.

Avoid holding on to broken items or appliances that you have no means to fix. Are there parts you can salvage instead? Maybe that broken retro toaster has cute metal feet or a beautiful early plastic bakelite handle you can put to use elsewhere.

Collecting can be a creative and enjoyable pastime, but hoarding is widely recognized as being bad for you and those who live with you. Trying to store too many things in your home can create a fire risk or cause unsanitary conditions that might ultimately pose a heath risk. Living in a constant state of mess is known to contribute to depression.

Try to get into the habit of always putting tools away after you have used them. This will save time and frustration later. Be considerate of others you live with and ensure that your projects do not spread into the shared spaces of the house or encroach on everyday living. At times you may need to spread a cloth and items to paint on the deck or at the back doorstep, but you don't want to be tripping over those same paint pots a week later. Likewise you might set up your sewing machine on the kitchen table, but it is not fair on those you live with for the machine to be left there indefinitely.

Get the basics sorted as you begin to enjoy many hours of satisfying reclaiming. Once you start you are likely to see the potential for creative projects all around you.

If your kitchen is a casual, warm and welcoming space it can be a place where ordinary moments become precious memories.

In the Kitchen

What features make the best kitchens? A well-proportioned space, with well-lit surfaces, essential implements within handy reach, and shelves stocked with ingredients, would surely inspire many of us to start cooking. But the best kitchens are more than simply a place to prepare food – they also provide a hub where members of the household can come together.

If your kitchen is a casual, warm and welcoming space it can be a place where ordinary moments become precious memories. As a mother of four children and seemingly always with a household full of friends and family, I have found that it is often while meals are being prepared or the dishes washed that some of the most significant and hilarious moments and conversations have occurred.

There are the dream kitchens we might one day enjoy – and then, for many of us, there are the homes we are living in, and the kitchens we are cooking in, right now. Are you feeling frustrated or bored with your kitchen's current look or layout? Start by making the most of what you have. With a bit of creativity there are plenty of upcycling options that can help improve both the style and functionality of this important room.

Transforming your kitchen doesn't have to entail demolishing everything and starting again. Are your kitchen cabinets sturdy but dull? Replacing cupboards can quickly become an expensive exercise, but if yours are of an older, solid wood style, they could be worth keeping. If flow is an issue, you might want to get a builder in to help reconfigure them into a smarter arrangement. Once sanded and repainted, they will likely last longer than their modern MDF equivalents. Some new, low-cost kitchens are made using plastic laminate board and have an intended lifecycle of no more than ten years. But if you are starting with solid wood cabinetry, a more cost-effective and planet-friendly long term option could be to refurbish and modernize the basic wooden frame rather than replace it with new cabinets made with lower quality materials.

Just because it is the kitchen it does not mean all cabinets need to be perfectly matched – or even fixed to the walls. One current trend is to make purpose-built kitchen cabinets look like pieces of furniture. Another is to use actual items of furniture, repurposed to suit your kitchen needs. Eclectic but functional storage spaces can be created by reclaiming a chest of drawers, bookshelves, industrial trolley or other non-kitchen piece for a design statement that adds personality. An added advantage is that you have the option of switching them out or taking them with you if you move.

I am often amazed at how something as simple as a whitewashing paint treatment can transform the look of a dull or overly-dark table or cabinet. I had the good fortune of picking up the cabinet (pictured left) for free after it was put out on the grass verge a few streets away from where I live. The cabinet was solid, with functioning doors and cute cavities where I suppose drawers used to be. I was sure it could fit into our home – it just needed a little tender loving care. Turn to page 174 to see how this cabinet and others looked in their original state, and a simple guide to how they were reclaimed.

Second hand dealers confirm the upswing in popularity of retro and vintage kitchenware over the past few years. Rather than precious china kept off-limits behind glass in old-fashioned display cabinets, the modern preference is for good-looking collectables that can be enjoyed on an everyday basis.

Perhaps your kitchen is perfectly functional, but lacking in personality. In that case maybe you could consider it to be a playground where you can collect and display a few of your favourite things. Use quirky or colorful crockery, retro appliances or jars of dry ingredients as decorative features.

The huge range of fabulous vintage and retro items available online or in retail stores can make your head spin. To keep the look of your kitchen cohesive, choose two or three colors and patterns, or keep to a range of tones, such as pastels, neutrals or brights. As always, look out for items that are well made or come from a reputable manufacturer. As an example, I have started collecting a range of crockery from a brand that was popular in in the 1950s and 1960s. Many second hand and thrift shops still stock a number of these pleasingly designed plates and cups, especially in provincial towns, where sometimes, entire house-lots get discarded because they are considered old fashioned. When on family car trips I find it hard not to stop at every small town charity store. Seizing the opportunities as I can, I have over the years, collected a beautiful – and mostly matching – set of crockery.

The success of inner-city second-hand dealers is due to the upswing in popularity of retro and vintage kitchenware over the past few years. Sought-after items include baking utensils, enamel mixing bowls, glass measuring jugs, hand beaters and stylish stove-top coffee pots. Rather than precious china kept off-limits behind glass in old-fashioned display cabinets, the modern preference is for good-looking collectables that can be enjoyed on an everyday basis.

An enduring kitchen trend is the use of open shelving for easy access and visual impact. Place curiosities and extra special items on high shelves where you can see them, but where they are safe from small or clumsy fingers, or the occasional flying ball.

Some extra care of vintage items can be required, but nothing should feel so precious that it can't be used – even if it is just for special occasions. Some extra care of vintage items can be required. Avoid putting old pieces or anything gilt-edged into the dishwasher as the hot water and strong detergents can wash away gold trim, or cause glazes to crack. Bone or wooden handled knives and other cooking implements are also best washed by hand as the rigours of the dishwasher can cause handles to discolor or crack, paint to flake or for wood to swell and become loose. Take care with your collectables but, if my experience is the measure, you also need to be prepared for a few breakages along the way. The ultimate kitchen is welcoming and relaxed; it is a vibrant hub, not a rarefied museum space.

Bigger doesn't always mean better when it comes to kitchen design. It can be a matter of using available space to better effect. No space for a pantry? Installing shallow open shelves can add a striking focal point as well as easy access, with an assortment of repurposed jars used to hold herbs, spices and cooking staples, see overleaf.

There is something very pleasing and tactile about glass. It has been used for decoration and as cups, bowls, plates, and storage bottles at least since Roman times. Beverages somehow taste better when sipped from glass, and it is universally appreciated for how it is smooth, cool to touch and sparkling in the light.

From reused containers, vintage kitchenware and the wood used to make cabinets, bench-tops and shelves, there are many ways materials can be upcycled in your kitchen.

Glass is inert, meaning its non-porous surface doesn't absorb food odors or germs. This makes it a far better material for storing food than plastic. In addition the transparency of a glass jar means you can see its contents at a glance. Glass is made from all-natural raw materials and it can be safely washed at high temperatures in the dishwasher.

Glass can be melted down and recycled repeatedly without losing its purity or quality, while glass that ends up in landfill can take tens of thousands of years to break down. There are many uses for leftover glass bottles and jars. Lidded glass jars can be used in the refrigerator to store leftover food. Once the lid is removed, food in a glass container can be reheated using a microwave or conventional oven. Hot food tastes better eaten from glass than food that has been reheated in a plastic container – and with none of the concerns regarding potential seepage by BPAs (bisphenol A).

My family have dispensed with conventional drinking glasses for everyday use, preferring to use small, recycled jars instead. They especially like that glass jars rarely break when dropped. Alternatively you can paint the lids of an assortment of glass jars to create a matching storage set, such as the one pictured left. See page 184 for more.

Glass can be melted down and recycled repeatedly without losing its purity or quality, while glass that ends up in landfill can take tens of thousands of years to break down. If you are disposing of unwanted and empty jars or bottles, you can pass on any that might be useful to your local charity shop and send the remainder to be recycled. Where I live, volunteers from a national charity fill empty jars with jams and chutney made with surplus fruit from orchards and private gardens. These are donated to local food banks.

Another natural and versatile material is wood. Solid wooden bench-tops (such as the bench-top pictured left) can easily be given a new lease of life through recoating and resealing. See page 172 for more on how this bench-top was given a whitewash paint effect.

Shopping for kitchen fittings can potentially be a little overwhelming. But considering an item's durability and longevity can help you weigh up the pros and cons. For instance, the vintage Smiths clock (pictured left) has classic Deco style and a face that is easy to read. This clock has been given a new glass face and converted to a quartz system for added functionality.

Visit your local second-hand furniture dealers' auction house or demolition yard to see what treasures can be had. Or try looking for rejects. The butler sink, left, was bought for a surprisingly low price from an online 'seconds' store. The green kitchen stool (pictured left) was given a new look using a crackle paint effect (see page 180 for more information on applying this handy paint technique).

Many beautiful kitchens have been crafted with repurposed industrial materials such as recycled steel, wooden cases, packing crates or laminated plywood.

In two of our previous homes we had kitchen cabinets and doors made out of plywood. In the first kitchen the cabinets were made to match a groovy retro stainless steel sink and tap unit I found at a demolition yard. I had to convince the cabinetmaker and the plumber that using these materials was a good idea. The second time around they were more easily persuaded. In my experience, tradespeople have typically been trained to rip out the old and replace it with the new. They can sometimes need a little encouragement to incorporate second hand or repurposed materials, but it is worth persisting – once on board, the best tradespeople will relish the opportunity to demonstrate their craft.

You can avoid ending up with more kitchenware items than you have space to store by deciding on a few styles or designs to collect. When rummaging through jumble-sale crockery, get in the habit of turning old plates and cups over and underneath you will see their mysterious – and often quite beautiful – marks and monograms. These small and sometimes cryptic symbols can provide clues as to a ceramic item's age, country of origin, factory and maker.

The manufacturer's marks on English china often include codes for shapes, dates, designers, artists and assistants. For example, pieces from Royal Doulton's Lambeth factory include monograms of the artists who worked on pieces together with alphabetical stamps of the young factory assistants. Crown Lynn (pictured here) is a range of everyday china from New Zealand that is growing increasingly collectable. It might be marked with the words Crown Lynn, a crown motif or simply a shape or number.

Learning to decipher these marks is to catch a tantalising glimpse into an object's past. With a bit of practice you will soon come to recognize the monograms of favorite crockery lines. This will help you to determine an item's collectability and to find the best buys at church fêtes, charity shops and garage sales.

OPPOSITE PAGE, CLOCKWISE FROM TOP RIGHT: Retro plates, a vintage enamel bowl and a wooden peeler adds yesteryear charm to kitchen tasks – in this instance dealing with a bumper crop of peaches; a collection of recycled bottles and caps are used to make homemade ginger beer and rhubarb fizzy drinks; a battered old enamel colander makes an ideal bench-top onion holder; assorted wooden spoons in a retro preserving jar; a collection of small recycled jars are ideal for storing herbs and spices – paper labels are fitted to the inside of each lid for identification.

Jam-making and filling old bottles with homemade fruit syrup is one of my favorite late-summer activities.

The kitchen can be a place of color and whimsy. I used my favorite 1950s blender to make a fresh fruit smoothie. Poured into recycled jars, repurposed as glasses and placed in an old wire milk-bottle caddy, we were then ready to head outside for an impromptu picnic.

Ample storage is vital in any kitchen, with generous pantry areas for food and other supplies. Too few cupboards, and you will feel their absence every time you return from the market and look for places to put things away. Kitchens benefit from clear surfaces, and here the cupboard is your friend, enabling you to impose order while stashing things tidily away for later.

Extra cupboard storage can be gained by attaching a shallow cabinet to the wall of an otherwise underutilized corner. The cabinet (pictured right) is an old wooden chest we bought online and mounted securely to a wall using builder's glue and long wooden screws. I wanted to paint the cabinet white so that it would fit with existing pieces of furniture in the kitchen, but I was also keen to preserve the chest's original character. Whitewashing provided an ideal compromise; it is a great way to revive an old piece of wooden furniture while leaving the wooden grain (and in this case also the chest's lettering) visible.

When whitewashing, apply a light coat of water-based white paint to the surface, and rub the surface all over with a damp cloth to achieve an opaque, even appearance. See page 172 for a step-by-step guide to simple whitewashing paint effects.

There are other simple ways to revamp cupboards. For instance, tired doors and handles can be replaced with smart new surfaces and knobs. Alternatively you might consider removing doors entirely to create an open-shelf effect. This is a clever way to transform high-mounted cupboards, which can often give a room a dated or overly closed-in feel.

Another revamping trick is to repaint the insides of your cabinets using a bright shade of paint. This provides a cheery pop of color every time you open the door. Choose a paint that is low in VOCs (volatile organic compounds). Enamel paints provide a hardwearing surface, and my preference is to use waterborne enamel, so as to also avoid introducing smelly and potentially toxic solvents near your food. See Tips and Tricks, page 162, for more information.

For the chest, left, I opted for a fresh white coat of high-gloss waterborne enamel for an easy-clean finish on shelves and the insides of the doors. For added interest I lined the back of the cupboard with samples of my favorite modern and vintage wallpapers.

How many moments do we spend each day with our head in a cupboard? This simple transformation offers you a small daily reward for time spent looking inside.

Sunlight and outdoor views help us to relax and reset our body clock to the natural rhythm of the day. Kitchens or the adjoining dining space often lead to a garden or deck, making them an ideal place to strengthen the link between the inside of your home and the outdoors. The wooden bi-folding doors (pictured overleaf) were bought from a demolition yard and repainted. They can be folded back on sunny days for easy flow inside and out.

The basic sideboard (pictured below) provides storage and a workable bench space. If made with solid timber, it will cope well with repeated splashes and knocks. See page 174 for details on how the cabinet below was upcycled from its original dowdy state.

Empty tin cans are an underutilized resource. Wash them thoroughly and run a can opener around the top to make sure no sharp bits are sticking up and then use them to hold cutlery and other kitchen items. Pop them into a wooden caddy to make easy trips from kitchen to table.

A Place to Lounge

The word lounge is a noun, but also a verb, suggesting by its very name a place to loll about in a leisurely and even a lazy fashion.

A Place to Lounge

The lounge provides a heart for your home; cozy in winter and cool in summer. It is welcoming, with comfortable furniture that encourages you to take time out to relax and socialize. The word lounge is a noun, but also a verb, suggesting by its very name a place to loll about in a leisurely and even a lazy fashion.

Comfort is key, but it is not the only element required in this room. The lounge is a 'living room'; a personal space reflecting your interests and personality, such as with well stocked bookshelves, photographs or pieces of art. At times the lounge also functions as a public space; as a parlor or a salon you can invite people into and where you feel comfortable entertaining. To this end a certain order needs to prevail in this room, including having places to put less attractive items out of view.

Retro pieces of furniture and collectables can be used to good effect in the lounge to make a style statement and add character. You can combine older pieces of furniture or decorative items with robust modern pieces for an eclectic effect. When choosing second hand furniture, look for signs of skilled workmanship, and the use of solid timber and quality fabrics. One test for a piece of furniture is to lift up one corner by the leg. The entire piece should remain rigid and retain its shape with minimal twisting. Check underneath to see if wooden parts have merely been glued or bolted together, or if they have been joined by a time-tested woodworking technique such as being mitred and doweled, dovetailed together or joined with a mortise and tenon.

Some items of furniture, such as the 1960s mustard-colored sofa (left) may still be structurally intact and not require a major facelift. Look out for colored accessories or other pieces of vintage furniture that compliment your piece. The use of a similar type of wood and the shape of the legs can be clues that items are from the same era. Interior styling options are endless and highly subjective – the fun is in playing around with different combinations and tweaking the look from one season to the next. In this instance, I matched the sofa with a freestanding red retro lamp, and for extra color added vintage yellow woolen blankets as cozy throws and matching furry cushions, found at a charity store.

To enjoy a living room that is cozy and warm but without skyrocketing heating bills, start your makeover with fundamentals such as insulation and draft prevention. You can draft-proof your lounge by checking doors and window frames for any gaps to plug. Repurposed sacking, vintage fabric or offcuts of new material can be upcycled into sausage-shaped, padded draft excluders that stop chilly blasts sneaking under the door.

You can significantly reduce heat loss through your lounge windows with double-glazing, or if that's beyond your budget, by using an old-fashioned solution: luxurious thick drapes. To be most effective, hang curtains full length, with a pelmet, or fabric cover, at the top, and sufficient material to puddle on the ground. The pelmet prevents warm air getting sucked out behind the curtain and fabric pooling on the floor prevents cold air falling from the windowpane and escaping around the curtain's base. Curtains benefit from having multiple layers, and can include an outer drape, an interior insulating layer and a lining. See page 152 for tips on adding extra warmth to your curtains.

As well as being cozy, the most appealing lounges reflect the personality of the household – their interests and experiences. Add character to the room with meaningful items or objets d'art, arranged out of harm's way along the top of a piano, mantelpiece, bookcase, high windowsill or shelf.

I like to fill quirky vintage dishes with star anise or similar spices for pleasant aromas and to naturally repel small insects. A simple way to add drama is with a tall arrangement of flowers or lichen-covered twigs.

A long thin sideboard is a classic piece of living room furniture that provides valuable storage and display space. Alternatively, a second-hand chest is ideal for stashing toys, board games and ugly but useful paraphernalia out of sight, as well as providing a flat top surface for stacked books and magazines.

Is your lounge suite comfortable and classically stylish, but looking a bit tired? If you have a well-designed old sofa or suite with a shape that you really love, it can be worth the investment to have it reupholstered in a new quality fabric of your choosing, rather than replacing it with a new model. An alternative is to cover the suite with loose fitted linen covers.

Sofa throws and cushions add extra color and comfort – and switch the mood of the room according to the season, or your whim. Using old buttons, woolen material from vintage blankets and fabric offcuts left over from upholstering the lounge suite, I made simple cushions in differing shapes and sizes (see right). Keep an eye out for interesting cushion covers in second-hand stores, or for fabric offcuts to sew yourself. Extra fabric with a soft texture can also be used to make a comforting throw for a chair or sofa, to help protect the chair's covering. See Things to sew, page 144, for more detail.

Large or heavy pieces of furniture with small or wheeled feet can potentially damage carpets or wooden floors. You can protect your carpet using vintage rubber or plastic bakelit furniture caster cups, or for an upcycled solution used small gold jar lids, upturned (see above, left).

Glass apothecary jars, bell jars, round glass vases and cloches are all ideal for displaying collections of small found objects; they look fabulous and save having to dust individual items. I discovered the lovely old bell jar with a ceramic base (pictured right) when I helped run a stall at a local school fair.

Framing items is another way to display treasures – and a good option when space is limited. See Frame it, page 132, for more ideas.

You can use color to give a coherent look to an assortment of different pieces of furniture – and to add an accent.

The room (left, and overleaf) is the lounge of a beach house we share with some old friends. The holiday house was furnished over time using things we have found or been given, plus some fairly haphazard second hand purchases. The lounge furniture was all made of cane, but as it had come from various sources it incorporated different styles ranging from dainty and round to square and chunky. The chairs and sofas had padded squabs covered in a variety of fabric covers, including a dated orange print. To achieve a more harmonious look we decided to paint all the cane chairs and two occasional tables in white.

Painting the furniture white had the immediate effect of connecting everything together visually. Draping a roll arm sofa in a loose white fabric coverslip made with unbleached calico helped it to fit the new look. White second-hand blinds and a bookshelf along one wall completed the ensemble. See page 65 for more.

The only piece of cane furniture not painted white was a two-seater sofa. This was instead painted in a bold accent color of turquoise. I picked the sofa as the feature piece because it was neither the smallest nor the largest item of furniture in the room, and because of its pretty shape. A handy guiding principle is to only paint something in a contrasting color if you consider it to be a feature worth highlighting.

Any object that is a different color from the rest is likely to be what you most notice when you first walk in to a room. This rule of thumb can also help you to determine when to use accent colors on skirting boards, doors and any feature walls.

While the cane furniture dried in the sun, I used the left over turquoise paint to color a wooden bowl we use for displaying shells. Then I re-covered the squabs, using a quantity of bone-colored stretch-cotton drill. Surplus outlet stores can be a cost-effective source of fabric and some retailers will offer an extra discount if you buy an entire roll, or bolt, at a time. It can sometimes be hard to estimate how much fabric you need for reupholstering projects, so it helps to have plenty of fabric to work with. I also made bright covers for our random assortment of scatter cushions and floor cushions. For this I used turquoise printed cotton fabric, in two patterns, with backings cut from a vintage woolen blanket.

RECLAIMING A SUITE OF CANE FURNITURE

You will need: 3–5 litres (6–10 pints) of white paint and an accent color of your choice. I used semi-gloss waterborne enamel, and 2 litres (4 pints) of turquoise paint to cover the two-seater sofa. You'll also need old paint brushes and a drop cloth, a bucket and a soft household brush.

How to: Use a bucket of water and a small brush to clean any dust from the furniture. Spread out the drop cloth and cover all surfaces with a generous coat of paint. You will need to dab the cane with the paintbrush to ensure full coverage. Allow to fully dry.

RECLAIMING CANE FURNITURE SQUABS (CUSHIONS)

You will need: A bolt of strong fabric (such as a cotton drill), sewing pins, a needle and cotton, scissors and a sewing machine.

How to: Lay out the fabric on the floor and use the existing squabs as a pattern when cutting the fabric to shape. Turn the fabric inside out and pin it to fit. Sew along three edges in a straight stich, leaving the forth edge open. Turn the fabric the right way around and check your sewn shape against the squab to ensure that it is the correct size and shape. Once you are happy with the fit, trim off any excess fabric and zigzag along any sewn edges.

Snip the material at right angles to the edge at the fabric corners to eliminate any puckers. Turn the fabric the right way round again and wriggle the squab into place inside it. Neatly fold any extra fabric at the open flap as you would fold the corners when wrapping a parcel with paper. Pin into place and hand sew along the remaining flap to close it up.

OPPOSITE PAGE, LEFT: The single cane chair (before and after) was repainted and its sponge squab was recovered. Scatter cushions in several prints help different shaped pieces of lounge furniture look like a set.

OPPOSITE PAGE, RIGHT: Color-blocking your books and other display items is an instant way to reduce visual clutter.

ABOVE: Add an eye-catching feature to a plain, backless set of shelves (above left) by adding a back panel and paint it in blocks of color. Arrange books by size and spine color and cluster similar complimentary knick-knacks together (above right).

A recent addition to the beach house lounge was a bright red beanbag, put out on the footpath by someone in our neighbourhood. The beanbag cover was in reasonable condition, however it was the wrong color for the rest of the decor. What it needed was a new cover over the top of the old red one. I found a large piece of tan-colored brushed cotton drill at a charity shop, but as there wasn't quite enough tan material to fully cover the beanbag, I added several panels of bone-colored fabric left over from covering the squabs.

RECLAIMING A BEAN BAG

You will need: Sufficient fabric depending on the size of the bag (approximately 3–4 metres (10–13 foot)), sewing pins, a needle and cotton, scissors and a sewing machine.

How to: Spread the fabric out on the floor and place the bean bag on top to use as a pattern for a loose cover. It can be a little tricky to cut a pattern from a three-dimensional shape, so allow a generous amount of fabric to start and be prepared to adjust the seams as required until you achieve a reasonable fit. Follow the same basic method used to cover the squabs (page 61), sewing all seams except for one, leaving an opening big enough to stuff the bean bag inside.

Once satisfied with the shape of your loose cover, trim off any excess fabric and zigzag along any sewn edges. Turn the fabric the right way round again and work the bean bag into place. Neatly fold any extra fabric at the open flap as you would fold the corners when wrapping a parcel with paper. Pin into place and hand sew along the remaining flap to close it up.

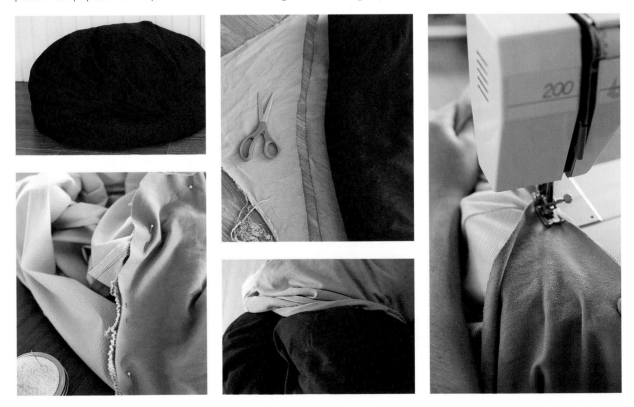

As a general rule, you can't go wrong furnishing your lounge if you choose well-made pieces, classic designs and natural fibers and textures. The best items of furniture have a style and standard of quality that lasts the distance, and can be mixed and matched over time, for a variety of different looks. There is an enduring appeal to pieces such as the vintage leather armchair, pictured above. Its classic style remains even when the chair is reduced to a dilapidated state.

The French armchair (left) dates from the 1950s and has been renovated using a variety of glues and leather fillers to patch holes and seal any cracks along the seams. Once patched and mended, the surface of a leather chair can be restored to a rich lustre by rubbing it with a beeswax-based leather polish. Any remaining imperfections, or patina, simply add to the chair's abundant character.

Treat your toes to a deep-piled floor woolen rug. Wool is the best choice of material for floor coverings, with unique natural qualities that help block heat loss through the floor. Studies have shown that wool carpet or floor rugs typically provide more warmth and trap less dust than synthetic alternatives. They also counteract any dampness in a room, as they can absorb moisture without feeling cold. Wool is a sustainable and fully biodegradable material and a vintage woolen rug is an investment. Even if it is a little threadbare by the time it comes to you, it will add instant old-world charm to any room.

Add flair to your lounge with a mix of old and upcycled items; the cocktail shaker, soda bottle and silver napkin rings (above, right) are all vintage pieces, while the gold vase (left) was made by painting the inside of an empty pickle jar using metallic paint and then filling it with foraged dried branches. See page 156 for a step-by-step guide to making the brown cushion (pictured left) using an old woolen cardigan.

Bedrooms

For some, a monotone color palette and a minimalist approach to furnishings feels most calming; for others, rich colors, layered textures and a scattering of personal effects conjures a more personal and intimate space.

Bedrooms

Of all the rooms in the house, the bedroom is where we spend the majority of our at-home hours. Granted, we are likely to be sleeping – or seeking sleep – for much of that time, which is why it is so important that our bedroom provides us with a relaxing haven. The ideal bedroom is not just calming and comfortable, but a healthy environment in which to spend our resting hours.

Generally speaking, the less clutter and unnecessary visual distraction in your bedroom the better, though personal preferences vary widely on this matter. For some, a monotone color palette and a spartan or minimalist approach to furnishings feels most calming; for others, rich colors, layered textures and a scattering of personal effects conjures a more intimate space. I have opted for a for a modern rustic look using natural textures, antiques and upcycled materials accented with muted color. Whatever interior style you choose, the best bedroom for you will be the one that feels like a personal sanctuary, a place where you can truly unwind and be re-energized.

Sleep specialists agree that good air quality is a key element if you are to enjoy an undisturbed night and wake feeling refreshed. A good place to start is with the fundamentals: a damp or draughty room is neither inviting nor healthy, so insulation and ventilation are priorities. Many homes have built-in ventilation systems that will help remove moisture and dust from a room, and you can help this by not introducing anything additional into your bedroom that is likely to undermine the air quality. This can include new furniture or synthetic fabrics that emit a strong artificial odor – that 'brand new smell' items often have when you first remove them from their plastic packaging.

New, mass-produced pieces of furniture might look stylish, but if they are made using medium-density fibreboard (MDF), laminates or other synthetic materials they may be giving off gas fumes. Such gases are often referred to as volatile organic compounds, or VOCs. Likewise, the materials used to make new fabrics are typically treated with chemicals during and after processing. This can include the fabric used to make clothing, bed linens and curtains. The chemical residue on such items can potentially be absorbed through skin contact, or inhaled directly. Some VOCs are dangerous to human health or cause harm to the environment, others are not acutely toxic, but are believed to have compounding long-term health effects.

A simple remedy is to wash any new clothes or bedding with an environmentally friendly laundry product before use – ideally-air drying the items outdoors rather than in a dryer. Pure wool carpets or rugs are also a good choice for floor covering. Studies have shown that a woolen carpet is more effective than synthetic carpet fibres for trapping impurities from the air, such as formaldehyde, nitrogen dioxide and sulphur dioxide.

Wherever possible, avoid the use of synthetic materials in your bedroom, and instead choose natural breathable fibers such as organic cotton, hemp, linen, jute and wool for bedding, drapes and floor coverings. Invest in high-thread count quality cotton or linen sheets and pillowcases for maximum comfort and longevity. Mix the luxurious with the simple; for instance, high-thread count cotton or linen sheets and pillowcases will deliver comfort and longevity, while a richly-colored vintage wool blanket, such as the one pictured, adds warmth and rustic style when used as a bedcovering.

Regular evening routines are essential for establishing healthy sleep patterns and for making a smooth nightly transition into sleep. Sleep experts also recommend reducing your exposure to bright artificial light, flickering screens and blue light in the period before bedtime.

Research suggests that exposure to artificial light after dusk and before bedtime suppresses the body's production of the hormone melatonin, and as melatonin regulates the sleep-wake cycle, a lack of it can reduce sleep quality. Sleep experts also recommend reducing your exposure to bright artificial light, flickering screens and blue light in the period before bedtime.

Ideally, we should refrain from looking at a computer screen, television or smartphone in the hour before hopping into bed. And when it comes to setting the mood of your bedroom, the soft glow of a low wattage bedside lamp is just the thing prior to bedtime to help prepare for sleep or romance. Personally, I love the simple functionality of the bedside light (pictured left), handmade by a local craftsman using repurposed timber from a bedhead, electric cord from an old appliance and an upside down mason jar.

The darker and quieter our bedrooms are during the night, the more likely we are to enjoy quality sleep. Sleep research suggests that exposure to light during our sleeping hours can also contribute to a range of negative health effects, including a greater risk of various cancers. Ideally, we should turn off all light-emitting gadgets and block any light from windows, before settling down to sleep.

Add an extra layer to the back of your existing bedroom curtains for warmth, and to block light or sound from outside. See page 152 for more detail.

It pays to take extra care when upcycling items of furniture for use in a bedroom to avoid using smelly paint, glue or mineral-based varnishes. But one of the many advantages of using antique or quality second hand furniture to furnish your home – and your bedroom in particular – is that any gasses from paint glue or varnish will have dissipated long ago. For instance, the old, black filing cabinet (pictured above) only needed a clean and a rub with beeswax-based polish before being repurposed as a deep-drawer bedside cabinet.

See page 170 for more on using low-VOC and environmentally-friendly products.

When it comes to setting the mood of your bedroom, the soft glow of a low-wattage bedside lamp is just the thing prior to bedtime to help prepare for sleep or romance.

One thing you need when dressing for the day is a decent mirror to see yourself in – and what better for an honest appraisal of your outfit than a free-standing, full-length mirror.

Sometimes it pays to ponder a little before embarking on an upcycling project. My initial idea, after acquiring this second-hand mirror, was that staining it black would be the best way to modernize it and add a little more elegance. I have found that black pieces of bedroom furniture combine well with natural-toned walls and crisp white bedding for a dramatic yet harmonious bedroom decor.

My next thought was to minimize some of the mirror's Victorian-style fussiness by reducing the height of the tall spindle mirror arms. This was done easily using a sharp handsaw. I also noticed that while the mirror surround, legs and arms were solid wood, the backing board was hardboard. Hardboard is made using compressed wood fibres and has been used in building and furniture since its invention in England in the late 1890s. It is functional, but not particularly attractive. I also noticed that the backing board was screwed on and realised it would be a simple matter to cover the backing board with fabric. By adding a fabric back, the mirror could also double as a decorative screen. Adding small wheels to the feet (taken from an old TV cabinet) completed the transformation.

RECLAIMING A FREE-STANDING MIRROR

You will need: 1 litre (2 pints) of water-based black wood stain, 1 medium sized paintbrush, masking tape, medium-to-light grade sandpaper, a drop cloth and clean lint-free rags.
For a fabric backing you need: Sufficient fabric to cover the backing board plus turnings, scissors, screwdriver and gaffer tape.

How to: Remove the mirror from its stand. Run a line of masking tape around the edge of the mirror to protect it from paint splashes and sandpaper scratches. Lightly sand all surfaces to be stained. Wipe off all dust with a clean just-damp cloth. Stain all wood surfaces with one or two coats as required to achieve the depth of tone you want. Allow the stain to fully dry between coats. Remove the masking tape and polish the mirror.

To cover a removable back panel with fabric, use a small hand screwdriver to undo all screws. Lay a piece of fabric right side down on the floor and place the backing panel on top. Cut the fabric roughly to shape, allowing extra material to fold over the edges on every side. As you pull the fabric tight and fold it over the edge, secure it in place using small strips of gaffer tape. Use the sharp end of your scissors to make a small hole in the fabric over each existing screw hole. Lay the mirror face down on the floor and put the fabric-backed panel on top. Line up the panel so you can reinsert all screws back into their original holes.

What better for an honest appraisal of your outfit
than a free-standing, full-length mirror.

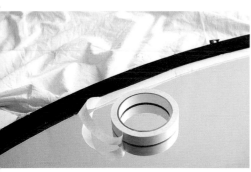

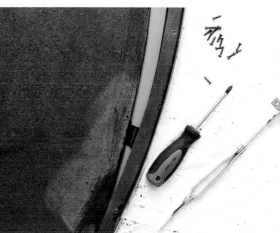

You can change the look of a bedroom by adding a dramatic wooden headboard. Don't worry if you are not an expert at working with wood. The modern rustic look incorporates rough wood finishes with imperfect edges and textures – making it a style that is very accommodating of basic woodworking skills. An example is this upcycled double headboard, which took a couple of hours to assemble using an assortment of timber offcuts, including bits of pallet wood and the remains of a broken single slat bed.

RECLAIMING A MIX-AND-MATCH WOODEN HEADBOARD

You will need: 4 lengths of wood 15 x 2.5 cm (6 x 1 in) and as long as you want your headboard to be tall, an assortment of wood between 2 and 5 cm (0.8 and 2 in) in thickness and in varying lengths, a sharp handsaw, drop saw or skill saw, a hammer and nails, self tapping screws and screwdriver. If you are painting your headboard, you will also need low-VOC paint in a color of your choice.

How to: Measure your bed base to determine how wide you wish your headboard to be. The headboard could be the same width as your bed, or wider to accommodate small shelves on each side. Lay out the four long lengths of wood vertically and evenly spaced to match the width of your bed base, allowing approximately 5 cm (2 in) overhang on each side. Lay your assorted bits of wood horizontally across the long lengths, starting with larger pieces and filling in any gaps with smaller pieces. Cut lengths to fit as required. You can lay all the boards flat, or add short pieces on their edge at either end, to create small shelves. Once assembled, sand off any rough edges. Leave the timber bare, or paint to suit.

I gave this headboard a rough coat of white paint that was light enough to allow different colors to show though and decided to leave it at that. For bedside lamps I chose two fabulous 1950s Jielde lamps, (the French equivalent of the Anglepoise lamp). We attached one lamp to the side of the headboard using a clamp, and screwed the other one into place, with a hole behind to feed the power cord though.

Upcycled pallet wood was also put to great effect when we gave this bland attic bedroom an upcycled makeover. The modern rustic look celebrates the use of natural materials such as roughly sawn timber. It is an ideal way to deal with scruffy or lacklustre spaces because rather than trying to hide rough surfaces and imperfect textures, it makes a feature of them.

The walls and ceilings of the attic bedroom are lined with hardboard (top left). One of the challenges with this old building material is that it cannot be plastered and sanded smooth. This is because the water component in plaster causes the hardboard to expand and throw the plaster off. The conventional approach to redecorating this space might be to rip out the hardboard and reline it with modern plasterboard, but instead we decided to make the most of the room's existing character and roughness by framing the ceiling and walls using thin strips of pallet wood. We used both vertical and horizontal strips to cover any unsightly joins and to create a more interesting paintable surface.

We minimized the visual impact of the walls and joinery by painting them all in the same off-white shade. We used remaining wood strips to create a highly textured feature wall – which we painted with selected color accents. The result was to turn a drab room into a dramatic one – without spending very much at all!

TO CREATE A TEXTURED FEATURE WALL

You will need: Assorted pallet wood, hammer, nails, pliers, screws and a pair of sturdy gloves, skill saw or drop saw, electric screwdriver, sandpaper and sugar soap, paint brushes, paint trays and a long-pile roller suitable for covering rough and textured surfaces.
To paint the walls: 10 litres (21 pints) of waterborne wall paint in a neutral shade, plus 1 litre (2 pints) each of any accent colors in low sheen waterborne enamel, in shades of your choice.
To paint the joinery: 1–2 litres (2–4 pints) of low sheen waterborne enamel in the same color as the walls.

How to: Using gloves, pliers and hammer, pull the wood pallets apart and remove any nails. Use lengths of pallet wood to cover any holes and to frame rough but paintable surfaces. Using the saw, cut timber strips to shape and nail or screw them onto your feature wall. For larger areas (such as along the bottom of the wall, left) you might save time and effort by using entire pallet sides in their existing form. Prepare walls and joinery for painting by lightly sanding them as necessary. Sweep away any dust and wash all surfaces using hot water and your favourite eco-friendly cleaner.

Paint all non-feature walls in low sheen wall paint and all joinery in a matching shade of waterborne enamel. Add any accent colors by lightly painting selected boards on your feature wall. For a co-ordinated look use any leftover paint to also paint some wooden boxes and a chair or other bedroom furniture.

The neutral-toned walls, joinery and flooring help focus attention on the richly textured feature wall, made with repurposed pallet wood.

A simple way to enjoy better air quality in your bedroom is to throw open your windows on fine days and let the fresh air circulate. You can also improve airflow in the bedroom by keeping the amount of furniture, and general bedroom clutter, to a minimum. If possible, also try to keep the space under your bed free. Using closed rather than open shelving will also help reduce dust and make cleaning easier. If your bedroom lacks built-in cupboards, a repurposed chest or upcycled cabinet can provide an elegant storage solution. You can also use wire basket sets and wooden crates, painted and stacked to store your personal effects or as a simple bedside cabinet (opposite page, bottom left and right).

Regularly clearing away bedroom clutter will also help maintain a calming space. Aim to eliminate anything in your bedroom that reminds you of work or that might potentially cause you stress. Keep the color palate of furniture and soft furnishings to a selected tonal range to make the space feel larger and less busy. One approach is to limit all large items of furniture to shades of white or black.

If space constraints mean you have to keep a computer, filing, bills or other such items in your bedroom, look out for a small roll-toped desk or shallow cabinet with doors you can use to easily shut everything out of sight. Clear away anything you do not need to keep on hand. For instance, you might repurpose an old chest in which to store excess bedding or out-of-season clothes and keep it elsewhere in the house, attic or garage.

Enjoying rustic style does not mean having to compromise on comfort. Mix the rough with a little bedroom luxury such as quality linen or cotton sheets, wool throws and velvet cushion covers (opposite page, middle).

Space to Create

Space to Create

Whether or not you work from home it can be useful to have some sort of home office. We don't all have the luxury to dedicate an entire room of the house to a study – but maybe a quiet corner is all you need. Once you understand your particular needs, it is possible to create an attractive and functional workspace in a surprisingly compact area.

The first step is to decide what you will be mostly using the space for. Is it a space for pursuing creative hobbies or a home office to be used for income-generating work? Do you need a clear desk area on which to spread out your things or are you mostly looking for somewhere quiet to write? Is it a place to pay bills and file away papers? Will you mostly be working on a laptop rather than a desk-based computer and if so, do you even need a desk? After considering how and where you prefer to work, you might identify your workplace as the kitchen table and your greatest need as being somewhere to tidily store away your papers, tools, stationery, fabric, wool or other crafting bits and bobs.

Take a walk around your home looking for possible spaces that could be better utilized. Is there a nook where you could put a small filing cabinet or desk – or a corner by a window where you might potentially write, read or simply sit and think? If space allows you could introduce a storage cabinet; alternatively, shelves might be a more compact option. Setting up a successful study corner starts with being open to the possibilities.

Before you buy any new pieces to furnish your space consider what you already have. Is any of your furniture currently underutilized that you could repurpose? You can make a cost-effective, creative and inspiring work area for yourself using upcycled and revamped pieces of office furniture and other simple elements. For instance, the table (pictured left) was created using basic, wooden trestle legs and old planks taken from a wooden pallet.

Keep an eye out for partially broken office chairs – or ones that look tatty but just need recovering. When companies are upgrading their office fittings and equipment, most will be only too happy to be rid of their unwanted junk. Set yourself up with office files and various lidded boxes to store your things. Many of these items can be simply made using repurposed items such as tin cans and cardboard boxes.

One item worth investing in is a vintage anglepoise lamp. They have classic style and enable you to direct light onto your desk when natural light is fading. Look for a lamp with a sturdy base or clamp you can attach to the edge of the table.

Make use of wall space to hang a pinboard or put up posters, framed pictures and inspiring quotes. Old maps are a great choice of wall adornment for any creative space. There is something universally pleasing about the look of old maps – and their suggestion of expansiveness and exploration can't help but fire the imagination.

Whatever your creative endeavor you are likely to have materials and tools that need to find a home. Aim to make your creative space as visually pleasing and as well-ordered as possible. Allow yourself ample storage for craft materials and unfinished projects. Establish some house rules for yourself and others. If your desk becomes a dumping spot for miscellaneous items it will not just look a mess – it will deter you from sitting down and using the space as you first intended. Have a place for everything; knowing the whereabouts of specific tools and materials saves time and minimizes frustration. Starting with clear surfaces and attractively ordered clutter will also help you to clear your thoughts and put you in a frame of mind to get creating.

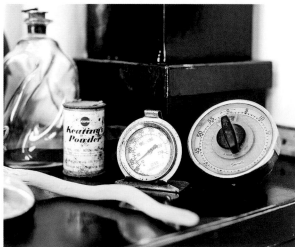

I am a big fan of old metal filing cabinets. With business documents increasingly being stored on company servers or in the cloud, physical filing equipment such as file boxes and metal cabinets are not needed in modern workplaces. Consequently you can often pick up second-hand filing cabinets online in an assortment of colors and sizes and at reasonable prices.

The deep drawers of old filing cabinets make them ideal for stowing away miscellaneous items. If you fill one draw with empty tins or cans, repurposed from the kitchen it is ideal for storing pens, drawing pencils, small tools or stationary items. Another drawer might be dedicated to a more conventional purpose, with files enabling you to keep on top of important paperwork. The tops of tall filing cabinets are perfect for whimsical collections of collectables.

Filing cabinets can be reclaimed using a variety of treatments. They can be sanded back for a brushed metal finish or coated in metallic or a bright gloss paint for a sharp new look. You can cluster several cabinets together for a pleasing effect and maximum storage. When I bought the tall black cabinet (pictured right), it was an insipid grey color. A coat of semi-gloss black paint transformed it completely. The vintage-looking drawer-labels complete the look – they were made using plain white card and given an instant vintage effect by painting them with cold black coffee.

Older cabinets such as the dark red and metallic cream cabinet from the 1950s (also pictured right) might just require a clean, rather than painting, so as not to obscure their original features.

You can create multiple places to sort and store your things. In the corner of my studio (pictured right) I clustered my red vintage filing cabinet with one I had upcycled. A heavy square, moulded glass vessel – originally a battery case – makes an attractive and stable container for long, rolled papers. A pair of small red cases, stacked, is handy for stowing away smaller items. The larger metal case was upcycled by a fairtrade collective using unwanted sheets of aluminium from a soft drink can factory. The other smaller red case was once my preschool lunch box! Yet more items are stored on the floor in an old wooden tea box I picked up in a kerbside collection, together with several old office file boxes that were being thrown out by a company I worked for some years ago.

It's amazing the difference a splash of color can make. I upcycled this home office ensemble after acquiring a boring old cream metal filing cabinet that was no longer required by a colleague. I teamed it with the ugliest-looking brown office chair. It had a ripped cover and I had rescued it some time earlier from a pile of junk outside an office block.

Being a successful upcycler involves learning to look past an object's initial dowdiness. Although the items looked shabby, the filing cabinet was sound and the drawer runners worked well. Likewise the chair, apart from its nasty color and torn cover, was also in good working order. It was a relatively simple matter to reclaim them both – giving them a snappy new look using a fresh coat of paint and a piece of bright red needlecord fabric.

A file folder to hold magazines was made using a cardboard box and some fabric remnants – with the leftover scraps used to make a matching pen holder. See page 98 for a step-by-step guide to making this.

A brightly-colored fabric-covered pinboard completes the space, providing a place to collect together inspiring images, quotes and other bits of ephemera. See page 102 for more.

RECLAIMING A METAL FILING CABINET

You will need: An old metal filing cabinet, light grade sandpaper, waterborne adhesive primer (sometimes known as Smooth Surface Sealer) gloss waterborne enamel in a shade of your choice and small to medium-sized paint brushes.

How to: Lightly sand the entire paintable surface of the filing cabinet. Wipe off any dust or debris and apply a light coat of waterborne adhesive primer. Use this product when painting smooth surfaces that might otherwise be tricky to paint. The adhesive primer will act as a grip coat helping the topcoat of paint to stick. Allow 24 hours for this coat to fully dry. Then use a waterborne enamel to paint the cabinet in a shade of your choice. I used a silvery metallic paint, applied with quick strokes using an old paintbrush, for a brushed metal look. Typically with metallic paints you first need a colored basecoat to achieve the metallic effect, but because I chose a metallic paint color similar to the cabinet, it was fine without it.

ABOVE RIGHT: This set of wheeled drawers started out life as a tool cabinet in a mechanic's garage. Cleaned up with a scrub and soapy water, it now provides the perfect place to store items for sewing and paper craft. A vintage suitcase that once belonged to my grandfather provides another place to stash materials away. You can add a rich gleam to an old leather or vinyl suitcase by cleaning all surfaces with a damp cloth then rubbing it with a natural beeswax-based polish.

RECLAIMING AN OFFICE CHAIR

You will need: A metal-framed office chair, light-grade sandpaper, waterborne adhesive primer, gloss waterborne enamel in a shade of your choice, small to medium sized paint brushes, a sewing machine, needles and cotton, approximately 2 metres (6.5 feet) of fabric, a hammer and upholstery tacks or a powerful staple gun.

How to: Unscrew any parts of the chair that can be taken apart to make painting and recovering more simple to achieve. (Take care to put the screws somewhere safe!) Lightly sand the entire paintable surface of the chair. Wipe off any dust or debris and apply a light coat of waterborne adhesive primer, allowing 24 hours for this coat to fully dry.

Paint the chair legs in a waterborne enamel in your chosen shade. I used a zingy orange to match the intensity of the red needlecord fabric. Allow the paint to fully dry before touching it up with a second coat and paint the wheels as required.

Measure your fabric against the parts of the chair that need recovering (opposite page, bottom left). Cut the fabric roughly to shape, making sure you have allowed plenty of extra material for seams. Turn the fabric inside out and pin to fit. Sew along any seams in a straight stich. Before you cut the fabric again, turn the fabric the right way around and check it is the correct size and shape. You may need to make some adjustments at this stage – taking in seams or letting them out a little, as required.

Once you are happy you have seams in the right place, trim off any excess fabric and zigzag along any sewn edges. Snip the material at right angles to the edge at the fabric corners. This helps eliminate puckers so the sewn cover can form a better shape around curves and corners.

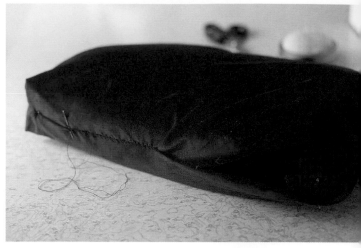

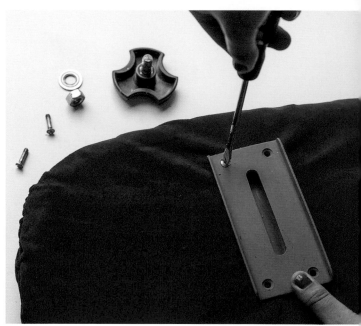

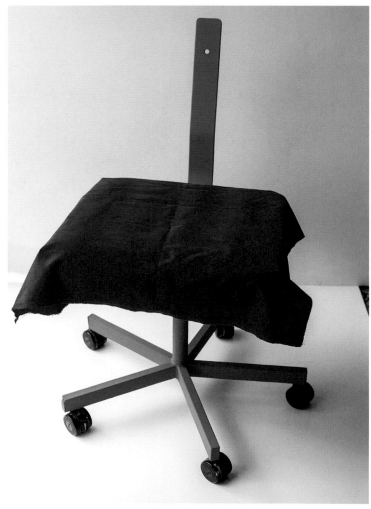

Turn the fabric the right way round again and fit it into place over the chair's back cushion. Neatly fold any extra fabric as you might fold the corners when wrapping a parcel with paper, then hand sew along the remaining flap to close it up.

Use your remaining fabric to spread upside down on a stool or table. Place your chair upside down on the fabric so the seat cushion is in the middle and you can pull the fabric up on each side of the seat and staple it into place. Cut to shape, allowing plenty of extra for folding along fabric edges and for stretching the fabric underneath the chair. Fold the fabric at each corner to make a neat edge (opposite page, bottom right).

Use a staple gun or hammer and small upholstery tacks to fix the fabric securely into place. Reassemble the various parts of the chair as necessary to complete.

BELOW: Gary the cat surveys the proceedings.

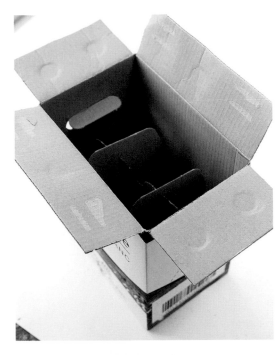

RECLAIMING A MAGAZINE OR FILE HOLDER

You wil need: A sturdy cardboard box with the length and width you require, sharp scissors, tape, sufficient fabric to cover the box, strong paper or fabric glue (such as white woodcraft glue), pen or dressmaker's chalk, an iron.

How to: Cut the top off the cardboard box to create the height and shape of your magazine or file holder (opposite page, bottom left). Create a tidy edge and add strength by covering all along the cut edge with tape. Fold it over into the inside of the box to form a tidy line. Lay out your fabric, right side down. Place your box on top and use your pen or dressmaker's chalk to mark the line to cut. Remember to allow enough fabric to turn approximately 5 cm (2 in) over along the edges. Snip the material at the corners (opposite page, centre).

Fold the material over along the edges and iron flat. Run a small bead of glue under the folded edge and press flat. Spread a thin layer of glue over the outside of the box and glue the fabric neatly into place (opposite page, bottom right). Once the glue is partly dry, use the iron to flatten the fabric edge against the cardboard. Allow the glue to fully dry before filling with magazines or files.

SIMPLE UPCYCLED DESK ACCESSORIES

Use any remaining fabric scraps to cover a clean, dry tin can. First run a can opener around the top edge of the tin to ensure there are no sharp bits sticking out. Cut the fabric to shape, allowing extra for turning over along edges. Iron flat. Run a small bead of glue under the folded edge and press flat. Spread a thin layer of glue over the tin and secure the fabric in place.

Create a place to store computer memory sticks or small stationery items by painting small cardboard boxes in matching shades. This is also a good way to use up small amounts of leftover paint (opposite page, middle right).

Clean, empty glass jars are easily turned into colorful containers for your desk by painting the glass on the inside. Apply an even coat and allow to fully dry. If you wish, you can add further embellishment by gluing a bead of cord or a scrap of lace around the outside of the jar. See pages 100–102.

A smart new pinboard completes your home office set up and is a surface where you can assemble a mix of whimsical images and other inspiring bits and bobs.

RECLAIMING A PINBOARD

You will need: A framed whiteboard or backed picture frame that is missing its glass, a piece of fabric slightly larger than your frame, light sandpaper, waterborne enamel paint in a shade of your choice, gaffer tape, strong paper or fabric glue, string and two metal eyelets and at least one sheet of thick corrugated cardboard. The cardboard needs to be thick enough to push drawing pins into it – I found the soft, yet thick, cardboard of an empty, flattened brown cardboard box to be ideal.

How to: Give the frame a quick light sand to prepare it for painting. Wipe off any dust and paint the frame using gloss waterborne enamel in a favorite shade. I used a zesty orange to match my upcycled office chair, teamed with a cheerful, red spotted fabric.

Cut the corrugated cardboard to fit inside the frame. Depending on the cardboard thickness you may need a second layer. Cut the fabric to a size than enables you to cover the cardboard completely on one side. Fold the extra fabric on the backside and secure it in place using a little gaffer tape.

Lay the picture frame down, right side up. Spread a generous amount of glue into the back of the picture frame and place the fabric-covered cardboard in place. Weigh it down with a few books or other heavy objects to help it dry flat. Allow to fully dry before removing weights. Attach eyelets and string for hanging your pinboard.

A bright fabric-covered pinboard adds a splash of color and provides a place to collect inspiring images, quotes, notes and other favorite bits of ephemera.

Stepping
Outside

Stepping Outside

Reclamation involves taking things that are broken, old and imperfect and giving them a new life – and the garden is the ideal place to experiment with this approach.

My favorite gardens are a combination of order and chaos. They are less about being perfectly weed-free and more about creating an outdoor space that feels loved; where fresh herbs, fruit and vegetables grow, children and bees are equally welcome and where a riot of plants can be allowed freedom to thrive. With some easy snacks and drinks, an old blanket and a few books you have everything you need for a lazy-day picnic on the lawn.

In my experience, gardening is a process of learning by trial and error. It takes patience, time – and inevitable mistakes. Along the way we can observe and enjoy the changing seasons, and learn to celebrate simple pleasures such as the beauty of asymmetry, the many subtle shades of nature and the ingenuous integrity of natural objects and processes.

Gardening teaches us how life is inextricably bound to plentiful water and healthy soil. A living, healthy garden is organic in its form and is always changing. Because the garden is an imperfect and forgiving place, it is somewhere you can let your imagination loose. You can experiment and change your mind. Just as you might transplant a shrub from one spot to another, or shift pots about at the beginning of a new season, you can also take away repurposed materials and reassemble them in other place.

Soon after moving into our current home I was happy to discover a cluster of old chimney bricks half buried in a gloomy corner of the garden. In the years since they have been moved a number of times around the property as we have developed our ideal garden layout.

Your use of various upcycled objects can also change with the season; runner beans might grow up and along tall bamboo poles or rustic wooden stakes, but you know it will only be a matter of time before you are pulling up the stakes along with the spent plants. If you find an old iron gate and wonder if it might be an even better object to train the beans along, there is always next year's crop to try it with.

There are many ways to incorporate salvaged items and jumble-sale finds into your garden. Look for rusty and rough objects with interesting shapes and textured surfaces that can be used to personalise your outdoor space or add color or character to a dull corner.

Stakes to secure young trees and train plants are always handy to have. Keep an eye out for unwanted plumbing pipes or other scrap metal objects that you can upcycle this way. It just involves looking at everyday objects in a different way and finding imaginative new uses for things.

Because reclamation involves pottering around with otherwise unwanted things, it can be very liberating. We can allow ourselves the freedom to take risks and experiment. It doesn't matter if we make mistakes. And in the process we can feel our confidence and our ability to be inventive steadily grow.

All sorts of objects can be repurposed as attractive planters, from rustic metal watering cans and washing tubs to old wheelbarrows. Simply use a hammer and nail to punch a few drainage holes in the bottom of battered and empty paint cans and fill them with potting mix and a selection of small plants.

Even smaller items can be used for windowsill planters, bringing a little garden into your kitchen. Large olive oil tins with interesting labels or aluminium pots and kettles make whimsical containers for living herbs and succulents. Windowsill planters are also handy for nursing small herbs and other seedlings not yet ready to be planted out.

Old pots can be bought at garage sales and given a completely new look with a quick coat of paint. You can also use paint to coordinate an assortment of random pots or to add a pop of color in dull corners.

One paint effect I have been playing around with lately is verdigris. The name comes from the Old French word *vert-de-Grèce*, meaning 'green of Greece'. Verdigris is the green or greenish-blue surface effect that naturally occurs over time when bronze, brass or copper is exposed to air or seawater and becomes weathered. It is typically seen on old metalwork and cast statues, and conjures images of grand European architecture, fabulous old statues and water features in stately gardens by the sea.

The verdigris touches in my garden are on a rather more humble scale – and achieved using a four-step paint effect that I found became easier to apply the more I experimented with it.

Our old wooden house came with an equally old garden – including some truly ancient, misshapen and unruly roses in dire need of training and support to stop them breaking in the wind. I have a lot to learn about looking after roses, but my first aim was not to kill these lovely old shrubs. I was so happy when I spied some spare metal piping and a curly metal bar stool in a roadside skip (see page 110, top left and top right). The metal was perfect for a verdigris paint makeover – and even better, with the bar seat unscrewed, the resulting four-pronged objet d'art and tall metal arch would provide just what I needed to help prop up one old rose and start training another into a more manageable shape. See pages 111–112.

You can potentially apply a verdigris effect to any paintable surface, but for the most convincing look it is best to limit your projects to outdoor items where verdigris naturally occurs, and to only apply the effect to surfaces that are, or could reasonably be, metal. A wrought iron garden table and chairs acquired a few years ago were looking a bit dull and dated so they became another ideal candidate for me to work on. See page 176 for more.

RECLAIMING METAL OR WROUGHT IRON WITH VERDIGRIS EFFECT

You will need: Discarded metal or wrought iron objects, sandpaper, wire brush, waterborne galvanised steel primer designed for use over galvanised steel and wrought iron, waterborne metallic paint in brown, gold or copper (for small items you can use test pots), paint in shades of blue and green, a little white paint, several medium sized paint brushes, an old toothbrush, a spray bottle filled with water and several old cloths.

How to: Sandpaper or wire brush over all surfaces to be painted. Wipe away any dust and prime the surface with waterborne exterior galvanized steel primer. Allow to fully dry. Add a coat of metallic paint in a shade of your choice and allow this to dry. Using a corner of an old cloth add alternate dabs of blue and green paint. Merge them together a little in places using a dry paintbrush or the cloth. Before the painted surface is fully dry, rub over with a dry (or if necessary a damp cloth), to soften the effect and reveal the metallic undertone in places.

You need to work quickly at this stage before the topcoat dries. Using an old toothbrush and a little white paint, watered down, flick on a few spots of white. Use your spray bottle to lightly spray the surface with water to create a drizzled effect. Either add more white flecks, or rub some off to get the look you want.

Once painted, I used the four-pronged metal object to support the main trunk of one old rose (below). A month later the garden had erupted in a riot of color.

My new metal arch (pictured left) proved to be just the thing to tie back a large old rose with huge thorns, that had previously grown way out of control – endangering itself and any unfortunates who wandered near.

Another fun upcycling project that gave me an opportunity to practice the verdigris paint effect was a dull old aluminium letterbox. I started by painting it with metallic copper for a bright undercoat, then followed the same steps as with the metal garden arches (see pages 110–111).

As well as trying different paint effects, you can also have a lot of fun experimenting with using color on garden furniture and pots. For instance the basic terracotta pots (below) are given an easy makeover using leftover blue house paint – adding a pop of color to a dull corner.

Second hand outdoor furniture can often be picked up for a reasonable price – or for free – when others are having a clear out. Wrought iron, steel, wood, cane – even plastic – furniture can all be successfully painted if you prepared the surface first and use quality paint. If you have are unsure about the correct undercoat or surface sealer to use, ask a specialist paint retailer.

When you find second hand metal furniture think of the potential as opposed to how it looks in its current state. Be brave in your color choices; the brighter light outdoors means that you can get away with more vivid shades and bolder combinations that you might choose for inside your home.

Do you have an outdoor area you can use for alfresco dining? You will be surprised how a coat of paint will breathe life into your new finds – and with a colorful assortment of tables and chairs at the ready, the garden can become a casual summer dining room. A wooden table protected with a coat or two of waterborne enamel, can subseqently be used outdoors.

The wooden outdoor table (pictured left and below) was updated from dull brown using stripes in yellow, green and blue pastels, and teamed with a mismatched collection of plastic chairs painted in the same colors.

Prepare the plastic chairs for painting by lightly sanding the entire surface area, especially over high-use spots such as arm rests. Paint with a light coat of waterborne enamel. Allow to fully dry before adding a second coat.

You can also repurpose an old metal wheelbarrow to create a colorful and compact garden kitchen garden for herbs and salad greens (see overleaf). Not only is a wheelbarrow garden easy to create, the fact that you can easily move it makes it ideal for small properties where space and sunny spots are at a premium. Position your mobile garden in a sheltered spot – and simply wheel it out of the way when you want to sit there yourself.

Check local garage sales or online trading sites for a reasonably-priced second-hand metal wheelbarrow. Look for a sturdy barrow with a decent weight-bearing wheel. Check the tire and rim are in good condition and that the handles are not rusty or loose. You can make the paint job as fancy as you like – or keep it simple and involve children in helping you. This is a perfect project for using up any leftover water-based enamel paint lurking about in your garage.

RECLAIMING A WHEELBARROW GARDEN

You will need: An old metal wheelbarrow, medium grade sandpaper, waterborne adhesive primer (sometimes called smooth surface sealer), gloss waterborne enamels in shades of your choice, small to medium-sized paint brushes, an electric drill, empty coffee sacks, small stones or gravel, potting mix and a selection of plants.

How to: If necessary, clean the barrow with soapy water and a scrubbing brush. Give all surfaces you wish to paint a quick sand.

Wipe off any dust and coat all surfaces with a light covering of waterborne adhesive primer. Allow to fully dry.

Top coat the barrow in colors of your choice. It is best to use waterborne enamels for a hardwearing result. I chose bright red and green, with handles and legs in a darker shade of green.

Once you have completed the painting and the barrow is dry, use an electric drill to make drainage holes in the base. Take care not to drill too many holes, or too near the corners, as it will weaken the barrow. Line the barrow with hemp sacking to provide a biodegradable and non-toxic layer between the barrow and the soil. Ask at your local cafe if they have empty fairtrade coffee sacks to give away or sell.

Cover the base with a layer of gravel for good drainage. Fill the barrow with potting mix and plant out with a mix of edibles and colorful flowers. Water well to fully soak the sack.

A kitchen garden in a barrow is the easiest way to start a new small vegetable garden. You don't even need lawn space to dig up – just park your barrow on the patio or deck and wheel it out of the way as space dictates.

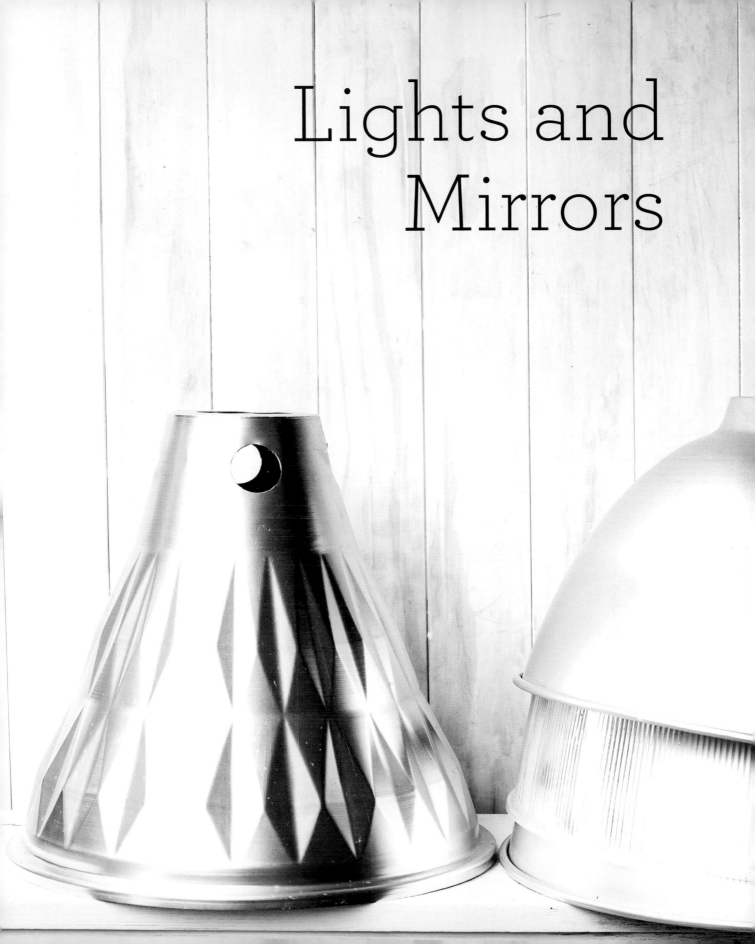

Lights and Mirrors

Lights and Mirrors

Decent lighting is integral to the successful functioning of any room. Light comes in various forms; depending on color and energy density it can have differing effects on our mood. The best light of all is natural light; warm sunlight baths a room in a cheerful glow, stimulates our bodies to produce vitamin D, helps regulate our circadian rhythms and is a factor in warding off depression.

It is worth considering how you might maximise your home's natural light – especially before undertaking a major home renovation project. Over the course of four different house refurbishments we have installed larger windows, enlarged door openings, replaced solid internal doors with glass panelled doors, added skylights and high windows, reconfigured kitchen sinks and benches, even turned a bedroom into a lounge – all to improve flow and access more natural light. It is amazing the positive impact on a room when even the smallest extra window is added, such as the narrow high window frame, pictured left.

If you are fortunate to live in a home or apartment with large and well-orientated windows it may be as simple as positioning furniture in order to make the most of the available sunlight. Well-designed curtains and blinds are ones that can be pulled right back to fully expose the window. Windows that are free of grime will let in the most sunlight possible – though that is often easier said than done. Cleverly positioned mirrors can also be used to reflect light and further brighten a room.

There will always be times, however, when you need to augment a room's natural light with artificial light – and this is where the fun begins. Whether modern or antique, lighting comes in two basic forms; fixed general, non-specific lighting, typically provided by a light, hung or mounted in the middle of the ceiling, and specific task lighting, using lamps or spotlights. Beyond that distinction, lamps, light shades and fittings come in all shapes and sizes. If you go hunting, a profusion of bold, classically designed and beautifully functional retro light shades and fittings can be found online and at quality second hand stores. As always, the trick is being able to visualize old things in a new setting.

One contemporary trend I particularly like is the use of oversized, industrial light fittings salvaged from factories and offices. A favorite cafe, located in a grand old building that was previously a post office, has a number of fabulous retro fittings, including giant globe lights originally from a town hall and similar but smaller round lights salvaged from an old dental practice that was being demolished. Industrial light shades can also be reclaimed to great effect in your home. It pays to match the scale of your light fittings to each room, but where space or high ceilings allow, extra large shades make an instant impact – as well as the practical consideration of allowing a greater amount of light to illuminate the room.

A profusion of bold, classically designed and beautifully functional retro light shades and fittings can be found online and at quality second hand stores. As always, the trick is being able to visualize old things in a new setting.

Considering a room's use and its particular lighting needs will help you to choose the best retro light fitting from the many options available. Does the room need brighter general, non-specific lighting or a dramatic pendant or chandelier as a focal point in the middle of the ceiling? Would the room's functionality be improved with specific task lighting, allowing you to direct concentrated bursts of light wherever it is most required. Anglepoise desk and floor lamps are one example of brilliantly functional task lighting. Originally designed in the 1930s to imitate the joints of a human arm, they allow great flexibility and ease of use.

OPPOSITE PAGE, RIGHT: The large metal dish of the ex-factory light shade provides effective illumination at the end of this long, gloomy hall.

ABOVE: A pendant light hung using a long cord, kept in place using an interesting old metal hook allows the light to be raised and lowered as required.

RIGHT: One of my best-ever roadside finds, this Italian-made chandelier adds a delicate elegance to a high-ceilinged room

Using a few simple tools and a fair bit of ingenuity, old lights and fittings can often be reconfigured and repurposed. Due care always needs to be taken with electricity and old appliances. If you have any concerns, have your upcycling project checked by a registered electrician to ensure it is safe to use.

In the case of the project pictured left, we started with the base and stand of a cheap modern freestanding lamp. The flimsy metal base was unstable and had gone rusty, but that aside, the wiring, power cord, central pole and top fitting were still all intact and functional. We added more substance by screwing on a round wooden disc underneath the existing base. Then we added a sturdy steel ring on top, adapted from a broken outdoor gas heater. The opaque plastic shade came from a large ex-factory pendant lamp, fixed to the pole using a wire frame from another broken lampshade. This beautiful lamp, pictured right, was the result.

OPPOSITE PAGE: This beautiful deco-esque lamp was made using reclaimed materials. Use an extra-large framed mirror leant against the floor or on top of a sturdy cabinet to reflect the ceiling space above.

LEFT AND BELOW: Look out for interestingly shaped mirrors in second hand stores.

The use of mirrors to reflect other surfaces and objects, bounce light around a room and create a greater sense of space are interior design tricks that have been employed in grand homes and halls for centuries. It is about conjuring a subtle illusion, an illusion d'optique – or trick of the light.

You can use the same techniques on a simpler scale in your own home. Place a mirror on a wall opposite a window to catch incoming light and bounce it across the room. Lean an extra-large framed mirror against the floor or on top of a sturdy cabinet rather than hanging it, so as to reflect the ceiling space above.

I love the shapes and time-worn patinas of retro and vintage mirrors and pick them up whenever I see one going for a bargain. Generally if you buy something you love, you will find a place for it – and living in an older house such as ours, not originally built to capture natural light, it is easy to find plenty of dark corners that benefit from the reflective sparkle of a strategically placed mirror.

When a lovely old Carlton Ware plate was dropped and broken a few years ago I resurrected the pieces by fixing them with tile adhesive around the edge of a small retro mirror, (opposite page, top left).

The bathroom is another space that can be made more fabulous with the use of mirrors. Typically bathrooms are small rooms, located on the less sunny side of a building. White walls and ceilings, and clever use of natural and artificial light can be used to create a bright and inviting room, stretching the space without the need for expensive renovation. Decent bathroom lighting also provides the very practical function of letting you see yourself clearly in the mirror.

A simple way to add drama to a bathroom is to add a feature wall in a vivid shade and hang a collection of vintage mirrors (see opposite page). A handmade rag rug, a crackle-painted chair and art painted on reclaimed wood blocks (below) complete the room.

Frame It

Frame It

What makes a house a home? Homeliness can be hard to define as its physical expression varies according to personal taste and preference. It is as much about atmosphere as it is about the details of interior decor. The word *gezellig*, which is core to Dutch culture but notoriously difficult to translate into English, perhaps comes closest to capturing the concept. A *gezellig* room is typically cozy and friendly, warm, safe and comfortable – everything that is enjoyably familiar or nostalgic. A *gezellig* atmosphere can be relaxed but also gregarious and filled with laughter. It can also be a moment of togetherness and shared understanding, where we enjoy a sense of connection and belonging.

Art is a key element in what makes a house feel like a home. By art, I don't just mean paintings, prints and photographs, but all decorative things, from a patterned quilt on a bed to the pleasing silhouette of a lamp. Art is an expression of creative skill and imagination. It may not provide a practical, or obvious, everyday function such as taps flowing with fresh water or chairs and tables we can sit at, but it makes an essential contribution to our psyche.

Like the playing of music or shelves lined with books, art – in all its forms – adds a layer of richness to daily life. Even a simple framed photograph or single piece of art hanging on a wall can help define the character of a room and extend something of the personality of the people living there.

Art prompts us to think about the things we cannot see, transporting us beyond the mundane and into the realm of emotion and ideas. Art can be sad and profound, but it can also help us make sense of the world by reminding us of things that cannot be understood with pure reason, such as love and beauty. Like music, art can make our homes more joyful, helping us to feel happier, calmer or more energized.

On a practical level, picture frames and shadow boxes provide a great way to preserve and display art, photographs and other treasured mementos. Done well, framing can help protect an image from dust, mildew and other potential damage. Framing can also serve a number of other important functions; the simple gesture of framing and displaying your child's artwork, for instance, is an expression of your love for them and affirms their creative efforts.

Modern living involves a fairly constant flow of things into our homes – and typically, not so many things being taken away. In order to impose a semblance of order and to maintain pleasant interior spaces, we need to regularly sort through our things and remove the dross.

Picture framing involves effort – and depending on the frame – some cost. Much as we might like to, we can't hold on to every item of art our children create, print every digital image we capture, or keep every interesting item of ephemera we find. We can use the process of choosing items to frame to determine what is most worth keeping.

When we enclose an image or object within a picture frame it defines it and gives it greater expression. Whether it is a child's drawing or a photograph capturing a special moment, choosing an item confirms that we value it enough to preserve and celebrate it. If you have held on to precious art or photographs with the intention of one day framing those items, you will know how very satisfying it is to finally hang them on a wall. Selecting the best things to frame allows us the freedom to get rid of other less significant items without guilt.

You can make the process of framing as simple or as complicated as you like, but understanding a few basic tips will help you to keep your framed items protected and look great when on display.

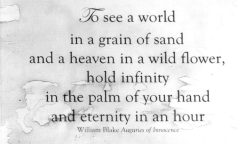

To see a world
in a grain of sand
and a heaven in a wild flower,
hold infinity
in the palm of your hand
and eternity in an hour

William Blake Auguries of Innocence

EARTH'S
CRAMMED
WITH
HEAVEN,
AND
EVERY
COMMON
BUSH
AFIRE
WITH
GOD

Elizabeth Barrett Browning

Custom framing can be very expensive – especially when framing larger items or using interesting frames. I always keep an eye out at charity stores and school fairs for sturdy frames. On several occasions I have bought a picture only for its frame and on closer inspection, decided I liked the picture enough to hang up as is.

Check that a frame is not loose at the corners and that the glass is not scratched or chipped. Missing glass can be replaced. If you consider a frame worthy of the extra cost, take your lovely old frame to a local glazier to have new glass cut to fit.

Matting or mount board is the stiff card that sits between the artwork and the glass. The use of mounts adds color, texture and depth. They also create an air space between the surface of the artwork and the glass, protecting it from smearing or condensation forming, and preventing photographs from sticking to the glass. Multiple mounts add greater depth, and extra thick ones create a three-dimensional, shadow-box effect.

If you are planning to cut new mounts or backing boards, enquire at a local printing firm and you may be able to source large sheets of offcut card or plastic board at no cost.

As a general rule of thumb, art on paper should always be framed under glass. Changes in humidity can cause exposed paper to buckle and warp, while airborne grease, dust and insects can cause damage. Oil paintings are generally not put under glass so the painting can breath and so as not to hide the subtleties of the surface texture and brushstrokes.

OPPOSITE PAGE LEFT: Favorite lines of poetry, printed out and washed with cold tea before being framed, together with vintage wallpaper. See also page 140.
BELOW: I was fascinated by the slightly menacing vintage children's wallpaper we discovered while renovating, so I mounted a piece directly onto the front of an empty frame and hung it in the room once lined with this paper.

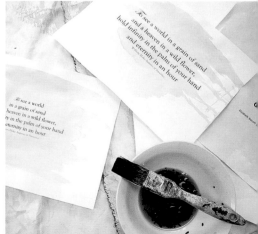

RECLAIMING AN OLD FRAME

You will need: A photograph, print or piece of artwork. A second hand picture frame that includes an outer frame, firm backing board (this can be masonite, plastic board, or stiff cardboard), a mat or mounting board cut to fit the artwork, glass cut to fit the frame, artist or masking tape, wide brown picture framing tape (or other sturdy tape such as gaffer tape), glazier points or tiny nails, small pliers and a hammer, strong cord or picture-hanging wire and wire-mounting hardware (such as D-ring hangers).

If you wish to paint the frame you will also need: Light sandpaper, paint, a dropcloth and a small or medium-sized paintbrush.

How to: Disassemble your frame by laying it front side down and removing the back tape and any pins. As you do this, notice of how the frame has been put together. This will vary depending on the age and quality.

Often, the back layer is brown craft paper used to cover up the inner workings. The next layer is typically a piece of foam core board, cardboard, or wood (in old frames) and is held in place with staples or tiny old nails. Use your pliers to gently remove these. Discard any staples or bent nails. If any old tiny nails remain usable, set them aside to reinsert when reassembling the frame.

Carefully take out the glass, wash it using warm soapy water and lay it on a tea towel to dry. Do not leave it on the floor to be stood on, as I have done rather regretfully in the past.

Your frame may only need a wash with warm soapy water. If it is an old timber frame try oiling it with a beeswax-based polish. If you want to paint the frame, lightly sand it before wiping off any dust. Lay the frame on the dropcloth and coat with paint, making sure you cover all edges that will be visible when hung. Allow to fully dry.

Lay the frame face down on a clean flat surface. Carefully lay the glass back into the frame and polish the surface of the glass facing you, using a clean, lint-free cloth.

Depending on their age, some second-hand frames come with mounts that are in good enough condition to re-use. Pre-cut mounts can be bought from a specialist picture framing or art supply store, or using a metal ruler, sharp craft knife and a steady hand, you can cut your own. If you are not keen on cutting the mount yourself, take your art and mount to a custom framing shop and for a small fee you can have it custom cut. Place the print or piece of art behind the mount with the portion of the image you wish to display showing through the hole in the mat. Secure in place using a strip of artist or masking tape along the top of the print or artwork.

Lay the mount face down on the clean glass. Before taping everything up, turn the piece of art over and check that the print or artwork is positioned correctly and that no lint is trapped between the art and the glass.

Carefully replace any clips or tiny nails back into the frame to hold the backing board and glass into place. Add more nails as necessary. If you want, cover the back again with paper. Finish by taping all around the edge using wide brown picture tape.

If your frame is missing its picture wire, screw in two D-ring hangers on either side of the frame, an equal distance from the top. Secure the picture wire or cord between both rings. Clean any stray fingerprints off the front of your now-framed art and it is ready to hang.

OPPOSITE PAGE, CLOCKWISE FROM TOP LEFT: Old frames are pulled apart and painted; while renovating we discovered multiple layers of old wallpaper lining an internal wall, these were carefully separated and used for a number of upcycling projects; favorite lines of poetry are printed and washed with cold tea before being framed, together with vintage wallpaper (see also page 138).

ABOVE: Precious fabric scraps from two of my great grandparent's sofas are framed in vintage frames I found in my parent's attic.

OPPOSITE PAGE: An annual Christmas poster from the 1920s is framed using an upcycled frame and vintage wallpaper as a backing panel; framing in an upcycled frame protects a selection of fragile and torn old tablecloths and other fine handiwork, passed down to me by my grandmother.

NATIVE FLOWERS OF NEW ZEALAND

NATIVE FLOWERS OF NEW ZEALAND

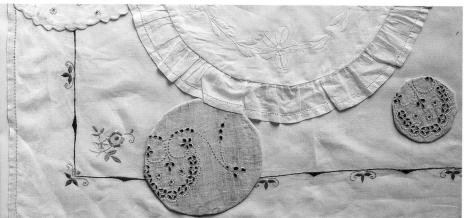

Things to Sew

Things to Sew

There is something very appealing about rows of colored bolts of fabric, neatly folded stacks of vintage textiles and the look and feel of bobbins wound with bright thread. Together they seem to represent so much possibility – but they can also look beautiful just as they are.

I remember as a young girl especially loving pearl-tipped pins, and being fascinated by the cryptic markings and rustle of brown tissue pattern paper, cards lined with silver domes and other mysterious articles of sewing paraphernalia stashed in my mother's wooden sewing cabinet. On childhood trips into town we would visit the haberdashery store, with its vast array of fabrics, multifarious button selection and seemingly endless rows of brown wooden cabinets with many small drawers, filled with all manner of items.

Even as an adult I still like the distinctive clunk made by a shop assistant's heavy metal sewing scissors as the blades slice cleanly though a piece of fabric. It reminds me of the sensation of using a sharp knife to split open the two halves of a ripe, juicy watermelon.

We may not have the time or the temperament for embroidery or other fine handicraft, but many of us find something fundamentally satisfying in the process of making. It is not unlike the pleasure you feel when harvesting fruit or vegetables you have grown yourself, or of wiping the last smears from a pan of still-hot homemade jam.

It is no coincidence that craft is widely used as a form of therapy for children and adults as a means of self-expression, developing fine motor skills and reducing stress. Studies suggest that knitting and other crafts can act as natural anti-depressants and can help protect our brains from aging. Sufferers of post-traumatic stress disorder have also used craft therapy to mitigate symptoms. It is not just the finished result that we find pleasing, it is the methodical nature of crafts such as knitting or crocheting, together with the look and feel of the materials that combine in a soothing and beneficial tactile experience.

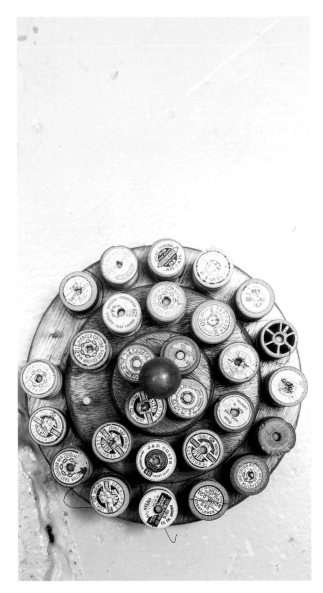

A sewing project using second hand material or fabric offcuts offers the extra satisfaction of making something out of nothing very much. It feels like an achievement to turn a roll of unremarkable surplus store fabric, some curtain tape and thread into a dramatic new set of curtains – and even better knowing you have done it for a fraction of what they might have cost, bought new. As with other reclamation projects, using second hand or repurposed materials also allows greater freedom to experiment, make mistakes and generally be more creative.

My family has included many craftswomen, including my sisters and my mother, as well as grandmothers, great-grandmothers and at least one great-aunt. The values of thrift, resourcefulness and a general attitude of 'make do and mend' can also be traced back through the various generations and family stories.

When I was about seven and we had just moved to a farm, my mother used an Epsom salts mix and a fair amount of scrubbing to cure a pile of fresh sheep skins that would otherwise have been thrown away. She cut and sewed the skins into a family set of warm fluffy slippers. My late grandmother always had a sewing or knitting project on the go and she made intricate lace using numerous tiny silver pins and interwoven white cotton bobbins well into her 80s.

I am too impatient to be an expert seamstress, but I do enjoy fixing a torn garment or whipping up a new set of curtains or bright cushion covers. Looking back I realize how many of my past creative projects have had an upcycling aspect. As teenagers, my sisters and I would often buy clothes at the Saturday morning flea market, then spend the afternoon altering the garments to suit us. We once cut and sewed our grandmother's old linen sheets into summer dresses because the fabric's texture and particular shade of off-white was a perfect match for some scraps of vintage white lace. I no longer have the clothes from that time, but I still wear a beautiful jet broach bought at the flea market by my oldest sister for the grand sum of 50 cents. And I have the skills that I acquired sorting through the jumble of goods for sale each week, and from picking apart and reassembling various items of clothing.

OPPOSITE PAGE, CLOCKWISE FROM TOP RIGHT: Delicate vintage pieces of handiwork can often be bought for a very small amount at second hand stores; tiny needles and a a lace-edged tablecloth crocheted by my grandmother and a cushion cover made by a sister; a spidery shall that was spun and crocheted by one of my sisters when she was 12 years old; another tablecloth crafted by one of my great-grandmothers; one of many doilies made by a family member.

My great-grandmother and great-aunt sewed and knitted, as many women of their generation did. They seem to have been prolific tablecloth and doily makers in particular. Doilies are highly intricate, small and often round mats for the table, typically made by crocheting, knitting or tatting fine cotton or linen thread. They were originally named after the fabric made by a 17th-century London draper called Doiley. Their main function was to protect the best Sunday furniture from scratches or marks. But they also provided women with the chance to showcase tiny samples of their nimblest handiwork.

A modern repurposing of these old doilies, such as framing them, or sewing them onto cushion covers or the front of bags or T-shirts, seems a fitting tribute to the creativity of these women from times past. See page 143 for one idea.

A sure way to add color and comfort to a room is with a fresh new set of curtains. Once you understand the mysteries of curtain tape and hooks, making your own curtains mostly involves sewing long straight seams and is easier than you might imagine. The curtains (opposite page, right) were sewn using thermal backed calico fabric and a tan fabric cut into long strips to create a colored edge. Both materials, as well as the curtain tape, were bought at a surplus goods store. Because these curtains cover large glass doors on the cold side of our house, I added an extra thermal backing using plain cream woolen blankets bought at various charity stores. Because I needed four blankets, it took me a few months to collect a set that matched. But then it was a relatively simple matter to take the curtains down and sew the blankets together and attach them to the inside of the curtains using a straight machine stich. Lastly I added some extra hooks to support the additional curtain weight. The difference the curtains make to the general warmth of the room during chilly winter months is significant.

Another trick for updating your existing curtains is by sewing a completely new piece of fabric to the front and treating the original curtain as the liner. Three quarter curtains rarely look good, and one way to add drama to a room is to add a new longer drop to the front of short curtains. For maximum thermal effect as well as light and sound blocking, generally the more curtain layers the better.

When we had our old lounge suit re-covered, I asked the upholsterer for the fabric scraps. Together with several metres of extra soft blue velvet and the cream wool of a vintage blanket, there was ample material to make a mix-and-match pile of cushions (bottom, left). The round cushions were fixed in the center using two large retro buttons. The plain velvet cushions were given an extra sewn seam around the outer edge as a cheat's form of piping. The cushions were filled with the re-fluffed inners of old pillows. The remaining square of blue velvet was backed with cream wool to make a soft sofa throw to help protect the sofa seat (middle left). A backing of woolen blanket fabric with a raw edge and pulled threads created a simple tasselled edging.

RECLAIM A MASON JAR TO MAKE A MINI SEWING KIT

Blanket scraps can be used to make a pin-cushioned topped sewing kit in a jar. This super cute sewing kit makes a handy gift for a family member who is leaving home or heading off to college.

You will need: A mason jar with metal screw band and metal disk. A small piece of thick fabric (approximately 30 x 30 cm (12 x 12 in), sewing pins, scissors, needle and cotton.
You will also need: Basic sewing materials to make up the kit; including scissors, black and white cotton and a packet of needles.

How to: Cut a rough circle of fabric, approximately 20cm (8 in) in diameter and set aside. Thread and knot a needle and cotton and set aside. Use smaller fabric offcuts to form a rounded shape with a slightly smaller diameter to the mason jar's metal disk. Place the rounded shape on the disk, right side up. Cover it with your fabric circle, gathering the edges of circle together on the underneath of the disk. Use the needle and cotton to gather together the edges of the circle. Trim off any extra fabric and sew the remaining edges down flat. Turn the padded circle over and push it firmly through the screw band. Fill the jar with the sewing materials and screw on the lid.

Turn tiny woolen blanket scraps or other suitably thick fabric into padded hearts, stitched around the edge using thick, colored embroidery thread (bottom left). Use the hearts as pincushions, or as rustic Christmas decorations.

RECLAIM A PAIR OF BOOT STUFFERS

Sick of your tall boots falling over in a scuffed heap? This is messy and potentially damaging for your boot's zips as they may be bent and twisted. These boot stuffers are easy to make using old magazines and bits of old blanket or other thick fabric. They are handy for your own wardrobe or as a gift for a friend.

You will need: Approximately 50 cm (20 in) of thick, fluffy material per pair of boot stuffers (old woolen blankets are perfect – and have lovely selvedges), string or two rubber bands, tape, several old magazines to the height you want the boot stuffers to be (A3 sized glossy real estate magazines are ideal for tall boots), thick cord (2 x 15cm (6 in), I used cord handles removed from a shopping bag), scissors, needle, cotton thread.

How to: Choose several old magazines that are the height you want your boot stuffers to be. Roll the magazines up tightly adding more layers of paper until they are thick enough to stand up and fit snugly inside the boot. Secure the magazine rolls at each end with tape.

Measure and cut 2 rectangles of material large enough to fit around each magazine roll, (first check the length against your magazine roll). Allow 3 cm (1.2 in) extra fabric at the top and bottom for turning over, and approximately 20 cm (8 in) of width to ensure you can roll the fabric around the magazine. If your material doesn't have a selvedge along the long end, allow extra width for also turning the fabric under along this edge.

Cut two small fabric squares 15 x 15 cm (6 x 6 in) and use to cover each end of the magazine roll. Secure using a rubber band or tightly tied string.

Lay out your rectangle of fabric, turning over approximately 3 cm (1.2 in) of fabric at top and bottom. The top and bottom of the fabric rectangle needs to line up to each end of the magazine roll. Pin or iron flat. Wrap the fabric around the magazine roll and pin into place. Use a needle and cotton to sew along all seams. Before you finish sewing around the top of each boot stuffer, tuck in a loop of cord and stich into place.

RECLAIM A CARDIGAN TO MAKE A CUSHION

Upcycle a favorite buttoned woolen cardigan or sweater to make a soft and cozy lounge cushion.

You will need: Buttoned cardigan or sweater, scissors, needle and cotton, cushion inners or old pillows, sewing machine threaded with matching cotton.

How to: Button up the cardigan and lay it out flat. Decide how big you intend the cushion to be. You may wish to match the size to your cushion inner. The one I made took two pillows to fill and is large enough to use on a couch or as a floor cushion. Cut off the cardigan arms. Turn the cardigan inside out and using the fabric from one arm, trim and pin it in place to fill the V-neck of the cardigan's front. Once the fabric has been pinned behind the front edge of the V-neck, use a straight stich to sew along the two sides of the V-neck.

With the cardigan still inside out, lay it out flat again and pin to mark straight edges and square corners to sew along (opposite page, bottom left).

Sew along all four edges, removing the pins as you go. Trim any extra fabric and zigzag along all four seams. Undo the buttons and turn the cardigan the right way out. Fill the cushion with the cushion inner. Do the buttons up again and trim off any loose threads.

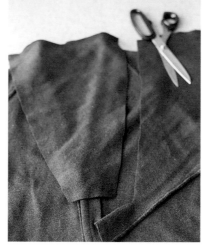

RECLAIM A SET OF OVEN MITTS

Fancy a fresh new set of oven mitts to use while baking? Upcycle a coffee sack and old woolen blanket fabric with this simple sewing project. You can pick up woolen blankets from charity shops and second hand stores. Empty coffee sacks are sometimes given away for free at cafes, or can be bought for a donation to charity or a minimal fee. Ask at your favourite local cafe that serves freshly ground fairtrade coffee.

You will need: Clean sacking material, woolen fabric (approximately 1 metre square (40 in sq)), sewing cotton to match your sacking and fabric, sewing scissors, an iron, a sewing machine threaded with a thick needle.

How to: Choose a clean sack with a texture that is not too stiff and with interesting words or patterns printed onto the fabric. Decide what size and shape you want your oven mitts to be. Remember to allow approximately 2 cm (0.8 in) along each edge for seams. I made mine a square shape 25 x 25 cm (10 x 10 in).

Cut two pieces of sacking to size. A raw edge of sacking fabric will fray easily, so start by zigzagging around the edges of your square.

Next cut your woolen blanket material to the same size. The mitts are best if you have double thickness of wool, so you need 4 squares of fabric the same size as the sacking squares. Also cut two rectangles of woolen fabric 15 x 4.5 cm (6 x 1.8 in) to make tabs.

Iron your woolen squares and rectangles so they are flat and smooth. To make the tabs, use a hot steam setting to iron the two rectangles with each side folded lengthwise into the middle, and then folded again. Iron flat. Sew along each folded tab, stitching approximately 5 mm (0.2 in) from the folded fabric edge.

Place your sacking square topside down onto the two pieces of woolen fabric. Pin together. Sew along the edge of 3 sides of the square, stitching 1–2 cm (0.4–0.8 in) from the folded fabric edge. Snip any extra fabric from across the corners and turn the mitt the right way out. You may need to use a blunt point such as the end of a wooden spoon handle to push out the corners.

Iron the mitt flat. Fold the two edges of the open side of the mitt into the inside of the mitt and iron flat. Take one tab and fold it in half. Poke it into the inside of the mitt to make a loop. Because of the thickness of the fabric it is best to place the two ends of the tab side by side. Pin in place.

Sew along the final edge of the mitt, securing the loops in place. Take care when sewing thick fabric to keep the sewing speed really slow – or you risk breaking your needle! Trim off any loose threads and you are done.

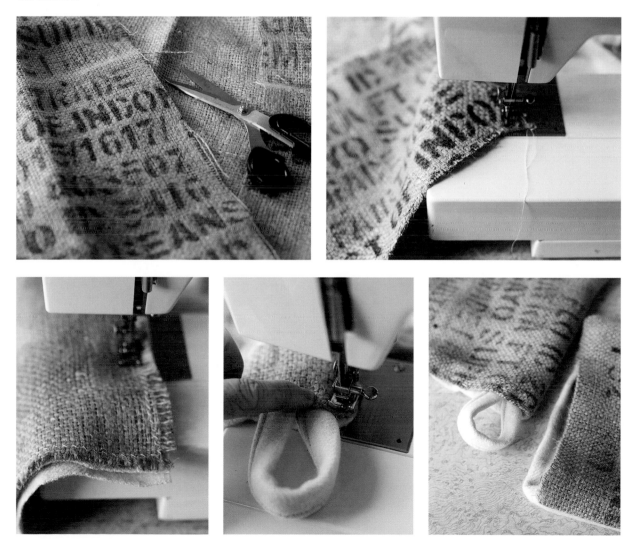

Easter celebrations at our
home start with steaming
Hot Cross Buns.

Tips and Tricks

Tips and Tricks

We know that charity stores and second hand shops are a fabulous place to find quirky treasures, and provide a feast for the eye. Less obviously, they can also be a great source of quality tools and other practical items.

You don't need a workshop stocked with expensive or specialist equipment to get started with upcycling, but you do need some key tools. It is amazing what can be achieved with a few simple hand tools, such as a handsaw, hammer and set of screwdrivers.

As with retro kitchenware there is a simple pleasure in using well-made, time-worn tools. In addition to the savings, it is also an appealing idea that classic tools might have been used in countless creative endeavors before yours. One of my favorite and frequently used tools is a short screwdriver, picked up a few years ago at a garage sale. The screwdriver is just as useful for opening a can of paint without damaging the rim as it is for undoing small flat-head screws. Its round wooden handle is smooth to touch and fits comfortably in the palm of my hand and the metal shank has been nicely burnished by time.

Keep an eye out at second hand stores and the like for basics such as pointy and snub-nosed metal pliers, sturdy wooden ladders and simple wood-working and picture-framing tools such as hammers of varying sizes as well as screwdrivers, planes, rasps and files. Look for screwdrivers and hammers made with quality steel and with handles that are comfortable to grip firmly. Avoid frustration when trying to remove screws by collecting a range of screwdrivers, including straight, Phillips and square heads of varying sizes and handle lengths. Short and stubby screwdrivers are handy for using inside awkward furniture corners. You can also get more driving force with a shorter distance between your hand and the point of the screwdriver.

Whether buying new or second hand, try to avoid cheap and nasty products. Lightness of weight can be an indicator that an item is made using poor grade steel. Another clue can be roughly cast plastic. If you are planning to do any kind of upholstery it is worth paying a little more for a quality and powerful staple gun. Check that it uses a standard sized staple. Cheap screwdrivers are often made out of soft metal, so when you push down hard on a stubborn screwhead, the tip strips out, making it useless. My preference, where possible, is to use a square head screwdriver and self-tapping square screws. A self-tapping screw drills its own hole as it is screwed in and the snugly fitting square head ensures they are easy to insert and, when necessary, undo again.

When removing screws, first check you are using the right shaped and sized blade to avoid stripping the screw head. For stubborn screws, fit the driver into the screw, put as much downward pressure as you can on the screwdriver, and hit the end with a hammer. This can sometimes pop the screw loose. It is also a trick to try with screws that have stripped out. A more aggressive solution for impossible screws is to drill out the screw head with a high-speed electric power drill. The downside is that while you have removed the head the body of the screw remains inside the timber. Before screwing a new screw into hardwood, first drill a small hole and put a little beeswax or soap on the threads of screws to make the screws drive more easily.

Adjustable spanners or wrenches and socket sets are all invaluable tools for undoing tricky nuts and bolts. Check for signs of wear and tear on the metal, such as corrosion or cracks. Any moving mechanisms need to be well oiled and rust free.

As you embark on more wide-ranging and ambitious reclamation projects, you may want to make use of more powerful tools. Electric sanders and drills can come in very handy when upcyling wooden furniture. If you intend to embark on projects that require some degree of carpentry or construction, then tools such as drop saws, circular saws, jigsaws and electric grinders can really speed up the task at hand. I find the electric grinder a useful but quite scary tool to use. As with other powerful tools, it requires earmuffs, safety goggles and absolute concentration on the task at hand.

It is possible to find decent second hand power tools at bargain prices, but is pays to first do a bit of research to familiarize yourself with quality brand names and to locate reputable second hand dealers. Pawn brokers or pawnshops can also be worth considering: typically they only buy items they know they will be able to sell easily, so won't carry poor-quality brands or stock faulty tools. Buying recognized brand name tools does not guarantee you will always get a good deal but it is a good place to start.

Basic hardware items such as sharp handsaws, gloves and dust masks typically all need to be bought new – as do perishables such as glues, paints and sandpaper. You might find such items if you happen to chance upon a garage sale by an elderly handyman who is divesting himself of his workshop. But even then, in case of products such as paints and glues, new is most likely to be better than old.

It might be hard to imagine now, but less than a century ago it was common for bright red paint to be made using mercury and for green paint to contain arsenic. Lead is one of ten chemicals of major public health concern, according to the World Health Organisation, but incredibly there are still places in the world where lead-based paint continues to be manufactured. Lead can potentially be found in really old paint, including the paint on old pieces of furniture. Lead paint is dangerous when it is being stripped or sanded. Sensible precautions when sanding older painted items include using a dust mask, doing your sanding in a well-ventilated area and to sweep up and dispose of any dust.

An alternative to sanding items that are potentially painted with lead-based paint – and one that I prefer – is to clean the surface with hot water and a grease-stripping product suitable for cleaning surfaces prior to painting or wallpapering. One such product is commonly known as sugar soap, or trisodium phosphate (TSP). You need to take care and use gloves when using this powerful cleaning product. As with painting, avoid tipping the waste-water down the drain as it can cause harm to marine life.

OPPOSITE PAGE, CLOCKWISE FROM TOP LEFT: Second hand stores are a reliable source of preserving equipment – there are also a multitude of unexpected upcycled uses for old preserving jars, such as the bedside lamp on page 72; recycling timber doesn't just reduce environmental impacts – it gives your home a sense of connection with buildings and furniture that have been used before (even humble pallet wood has many uses, including a simple bedhead or paneling for a rustic feature wall); vintage woolen rugs can be used as sofa throws, bedspreads, as picnic blankets, or used in various sewing projects; a selection of second hand woodworking tools; fairtrade coffee bean sacks are biodegradable and natural, making them a useful resource for use in the garden.

ABOVE: You can help revive tired old paintbrushes by boiling them in water mixed with white vinegar. Lay the bristles flat to dry.

When painting, it is worth investing in top-quality paint products in order to achieve a good result that lasts. Also, look for paint brands with environmental credentials certified by an independent third party and ones that offer a range of 'VOC free' and 'low VOC' products. Volatile organic compounds, (VOCs), can be artificially made or naturally occurring and emit toxic gasses at room temperature. As mentioned in Bedrooms, page 71, some VOCs are dangerous to human health or cause harm to the environment, others are not acutely toxic, but are believed to have compounding long-term health effects.

Solvent or oil-based, paints are examples of products with high levels of VOCs. Turpentine or white spirit is another example; you only need to undo the lid to smell a strong odor. Avoid solvent-based products where possible. There are some instances when a solvent-based product will deliver a more durable paint finish, but in most cases a good quality water-based or waterborne product will suffice.

In my experience, water-based paints are far easier to apply than solvent-based equivalents. They are also simpler to clean. A simple way to check which paint is which is to look at the cleaning instructions on the label. Solvent-based paints need to be cleaned with white spirit or turpentine, while water-based paints can be cleaned with warm, soapy water or a medium pressure hose.

Look for a spray gun fitting to attach to your regular garden hose. These are widely available at hardware and big stores. Once fitted to your hose the nozzle becomes a water blaster and you can use the water pressure to quickly and easily clean your paintbrushes – it is also ideal for cleaning various second hand items before upcycling. An advantage of cleaning your paintbrushes this way is that any waste-water can simply spray onto your lawn and dissipate through the grass.

Various whitewash paint effects can be applied to solid timber kitchen benches as well as wooden furniture in order to create practical working surfaces with bucket loads of character.

RECLAIM A WOODEN BENCH

Horizontal surfaces such as the kitchen benchtop (opposite page, top left), have a huge visual impact on a room. Painting the plain solid wooden bench white instantly made this kitchen seem much larger and lighter than it had previously. The beauty of a whitewash paint effect is that you get the impact of white, while retaining some of the character of the wood underneath – and it is wonderfully imperfect!

You will need: A timber surface, sanded smooth, gloves, soft cloth or old sock, various paint brushes, depending on the size of your bench approximately 1 liter (2 pints) of semi-gloss waterborne enamel in a color of your choice.

For the sealer: Depending on the use of the bench you might choose one of several options. An environmentally-friendly waterborne urethane varnish in a satin finish is easy to apply, dries clear and creates a sealed workable surface suitable for a table or buffet benchtop. For heavy use areas that get wet on a regular basis (such as near a sink) choose a clear polyurethane product. Typically, these solvent-based products are smelly when drying and can dry with a slight yellow tinge

How to: Ensure your timber surface is clean and sanded smooth. Lightly paint one area using a little paint and fast-sweeping strokes following the line of the wood grain. Feather the paint edges, so when you move to the next areas you can blend the paint together smoothly.

Rub over the painted areas using a dry paintbrush, an old sock stretched over your hand or a damp cloth for a softer, more even effect. Work fast over the surface as the paint will soak in quickly. If one part has too much paint, remove some of it using a pot-scouring cloth and a little water (opposite page, middle left).

Once you have achieved the effect you want, move to the next unpainted area.

Once the surface is fully dry, apply several coats of your chosen sealer, per the product instructions (opposite page, bottom left). Allow to fully dry between coats and before use.

It can be quite astounding the difference a coat of rough white paint will do to an otherwise drab piece of furniture. The solid wood dresser (opposite page top, left) was initially bought second hand to use as a kitchen hutch dresser. As I am relatively short, I decided the upper drawers would be better removed to create more open shelf space.

After a rough sand all over, the cabinet was painted with a light coat of ivory-colored waterbased enamel paint that was diluted with extra water (opposite page, top right). When the coat of paint was just dry, it was sanded back in places to create a rustic, farmhouse kitchen effect. For a convincing look, sand back the places that might normally get the most wear and tear, such as handles, corners and along any raised edges.

The sideboard (opposite page, bottom left) was picked up for free from a roadside verge. The backing board is hardboard, but the rest of the cabinet is constructed with solid wood. Its drawers were already missing and the black panel at the front seemed to serve no purpose, so it was removed. The cabinet needed a decent scrub with soapy water. We used a screwdriver to remove the door handles before lightly sanding the entire surface. Then the cabinet was lightly painted with white waterborne enamel in a matt finish. I used an old paintbrush and quick brush strokes to create a rough effect. Once fully dry, the handles were put back on and the cabinet was put to use. See page 51 for more.

Wooden outdoor tables provide an ideal surface to experiment with paint effects and color combinations. You can add more layers or rub them back until you get a look you like.

This table and chair set was in dire need of a refresh – the solution (pictured right) was to paint it green, with a verdigris paint effect on the chairs and table legs.

First the tabletop was sanded back to bare wood and undercoated in white. Once this had fully dried, the table was painted with a bright green waterborne enamel coat to help seal and protect the wood. When the enamel coat was dry a light coating of turquoise paint was applied over the top. I rubbed the bright turquoise layer back in places using a clean, lint-free cloth, and following the direction of the wood grain. After this coat dried, I added some darker green, using a dry brush and a minimum covering of paint. This time I did not follow the direction of the wood grain, but dragged the brush back and forth in a haphazard fashion. Before the dark green had fully dried, I added a few swipes of charcoal-colored paint following the wood grain again. By the time I was finished, the cloth was well camouflaged with the table!

The verdigris paint effect on the chairs and table legs was created using alternate dabs or strokes of blue and green paint. Before the paint dries, merge them together a little to soften the effect, using a dry cloth. Once this layer has almost fully dried, use a paintbrush and a little white paint to flick on a few spots of white. I lightly sprayed the metalwork with the garden hose to create a drizzled effect. Allow to fully dry. See pages 108–113 for more.

It is not always about adding paint to get a new look. This wooden cabinet was picked up from a family who were moving and had filled a skip with things that were free to be taken away. The cabinet is solid wood, but the back is made with hardboard, marked from a little water damage. One corner of the cabinet showed signs of borer damage, so as a precaution, this was treated before I brought the bookshelf into my studio.

'Borer' can also be known as furniture beetle, woodworm beetle or bora beetle. The larvae feed on timber and tunnel out to breed and die. You can treat borer in various ways, including using a fumigator bomb, dips and sprays applied directly onto the wood. These products can be bought from general hardware stores.

This bookcase did not seem to have been varnished, so instead of sanding it, I scrubbed it with sugar soap (see page 167 for more detail) and once fully dry, oiled it with a generous layer of beeswax-based natural furniture polish. The look of the hardboard back was a little dull, so I cut two strips of black velour and glued them into place using white carpenter's glue. Velour is fake velvet, it was ideal for this project because its raw edges do not fray.

Crackle paint is lots of fun to use and is perfect when you want to add character to an item. The more crackle paint you apply in any one spot, the deeper the cracks will be. Once the crackle is dry, apply a quick topcoat in a contrasting color; I chose an antique cream. The crackle layer lifts and cracks, revealing the base color underneath. The crackle medium reacts very quickly with the topcoat, you cannot go back over areas you have already painted once the crackling has started, as the paint will lift in nasty blobs.

RECLAIM A SET OF WOODEN CHAIRS

Sometimes it's about what you take away rather than what you add that makes all the difference. The basic steel and laminated wooden school chairs (pictured opposite page, bottom) came my way after friends cleaned out a church hall basement. Of classic design and solid construction, they were still sturdy despite many years of use. The chairs are not all the same design – so my aim was to tidy them up as well as giving them some sort of treatment that would help them look more unified. A bit of elbow grease turned the four tatty old school chairs into a stylishly understated set.

Rather than paint the chairs I decided to strip the metal back before sealing it, with a clear sealer, to prevent it from rusting back up again. The wood was also sanded back and sealed to reveal some lovely grain. All the hand sanding made for a few hours of work (approximately 1 hour per chair), but if done while sitting in the sun and listening to history podcasts is not an unpleasant way to while away the time.

You will need: Old metal and wooden school chairs, light to medium grade sandpaper, clear matt sealer – suitable for wood, clear semi-gloss sealer – suitable for metal (this will likely be a two-pot solvent-based product), small- to medium-sized paintbrushes, mineral turpentine, several clean cloth rags and masking tape.

How to: Lightly sand the entire wooden surface of the chair. I also chose to sand back the metal parts completely, which added considerably to the sanding time, but made a huge difference to the final look (see overleaf). Clean off any dust or debris using a damp rag or cloth. At the points where the metal and wood parts come together, cover the metalwork with masking tape.

Apply a light coat of clear matt sealer to the wood. Allow to dry completely before lightly sanding, wiping clean with a dry cloth and applying a second coat, and if necessary a third coat, to achieve the finish you want.

Once the final coat of wood sealer is fully dry, remove the masking tape from the metal and coat the metalwork with one coat of metal sealer.

The old school chairs make comfortable kitchen dining chairs and compliment this small retro wood and formica table – another favorite saved-from-the-dump find.

OPPOSITE PAGE, TOP RIGHT: This chair was picked up on the side of the road a few years back. The base was broken so I replaced it using a scrap piece of hardboard, cut to shape using an electric jigsaw. The new base was painted brown to match the original wood. Then I gave the chair a crackle effect, to add interest and disguise the chair's new base.

OPPOSITE PAGE, BOTTOM: Old school chairs await a makeover.

OVERLEAF: Once upcycled, the old school chairs make comfortable kitchen dining chairs and compliment the retro wood and formica table – another favorite saved-from-the-dump find.

You can make an assortment of glass bottles look like a set by simply painting the lids the same color (opposite page, left).

I chose to paint my kitchen jar lids in a glossy black. The trick is not to get any paint on the inside of the lids, so as not to taint the flavor of the ingredients stored in the jar.

The best way to do this is to first paint the tops of the lids and leave them to fully dry. Next, hold the lids between your thumb and your index or middle fingers and carefully paint around the edge and bottom lip of the jar lid. Lay the lids on their backs (which were painted first and are now dry), allowing the remainder of the paint to fully dry.

It is so satisfying when you get an idea for using an object in a completely different way. Assorted demolition yard latches are mounted on a painted board to create a series of hooks (top right). A rack such as this can be used in the bathroom, bedroom or kitchen – wherever you want to hang cloths or clothes.

A broken, oversized pepper grinder was reinvented by removing the internal parts and painting the wooden body with silver metallic paint to make a giant candlestick (bottom, right).

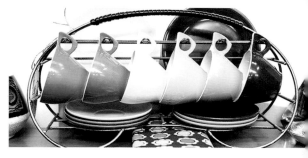

There is no shortage of fabulous yesteryear goods, demolition-yard building materials and charming charity shop miscellanea to be discovered. Just because a household object or item of furniture has been discarded by someone else does not necessarily mean it is a piece of junk. In each instance let the quality of the item – and your discerning eye – be your guide.

Resources

Flea markets, car boot sales, charity stores, school fundraising fairs and street markets can all be great places to find collectibles, vintage homewares and other items to upcycle. Look out for posters advertising local events or search online for local charity stores listings and weekend garage sales in your area.

Auction houses and demolition yards are other places to pick up pre-loved furniture and building materials with character. Reputable pawn shops can be a good place to look for second hand tools. Check online for local listings.

There are many online trading sites where you can buy and sell secondhand items, including Ebay in the UK (ebay.co.uk), Craigslist in the US (craigslist.org), Gumtree (gumtree.com.au) and Ebay Australia (ebay.com.au) in Australia and Trade Me (trademe.co.nz) in New Zealand. Craigslist is divided into locally based mini websites, so all transactions are based in your area, and other sites, such as Gumtree and Trade Me, allow searching by region.

A number of websites offer free items. It pays to stick to local or well-established online networks, and to be wary of websites where you have to provide personal detail in order to access free things. The Freecycle Network (freecycle.org) is an example of a nonprofit network with thousands of groups around the world helping people give and receive free items within their local area.

USA

BRIMFIELD ANTIQUE SHOW
Held along a one-mile stretch of Route 20 in Brimfield, Massachusetts, this huge event features 6,000 dealers offering everything from old lighting fixtures, estate silver and Early American furniture. Held several times a year. brimfieldshow.comBrooklyn Flea

A busy weekly New York City market features pottery, midcentury furniture, and vintage home accessories and more. brooklynflea.com

GOODWILL THRIFT STORES
A huge network of more than 3,000 retail thrift stores in the United States and Canada, run by the nonprofit organization Goodwill Industries. shopgoodwill.com

SPRINGFIELD ANTIQUE SHOW
4401 S Charleston Pike, Springfield, Ohio, OH 45502. This show is held the third weekend of most months and attracts up to 2,500 vendors to the fairgrounds. Likely finds: advertising signs, Midwestern pottery, vintage fashion, and painted furniture. springfieldantiqueshow.com

UK

ANNIE SLOAN
UK designer Annie Sloan's range of chalk paint can be used on just about any surface, including wood, concrete, metal, matt plastic, earthenware and more. anniesloan.com

BRITISH HEART FOUNDATION FURNITURE AND ELECTRICAL STORES
More than 700 shops around the UK including over 170 dedicated Furniture and Electrical shops makes them one of the biggest furniture retailers in the UK. An ideal place to find well priced antique or retro gems. bhf.org.uk

LASSCO
An established source of architectural antiques, salvaged building materials, art and curiosities. Expensive but worth a look. lassco.co.uk

THE MALVERN FLEA AND COLLECTORS FAIR
Three Counties Showground, Great Malvern. Vintage and antiques fairs are among the best places to find bargains, design classics and retro kitsch. This fair is considered one of the best and is held up to 10 times a year. b2bevents.info

PETERBOROUGH FESTIVAL OF ANTIQUES
East of England Showground. This fair is held twice yearly and is one the largest of its kind in England. bobevansfairs.co.uk

RETROUVIUS
1016 Harrow Road, Kensal Green, London NW10 5NS. A warehouse of diverse stock ranging from architectural salvage and other demolition materials to quirky collectibles and pieces of modernist furniture. retrouvius.com

SALVO

A national directory of dealers of antique, salvage and reclaimed goods. salvo.co.uk

AUSTRALIA

THE BOWER RE-USE AND REPAIR CENTRE

142 Addison Road, Marrickville, New South Wales 2004. A registered not-for-profit co-operative and charity selling pre-loved household, building and office goods. The Bower's primary aim is to reduce waste by diverting re-usable household and office items back to the community at affordable prices. canterbury.nsw.gov.au

BROTHERHOOD OF ST LAURENCE

The Brotherhood of St Laurence is a not-for-profit working towards a poverty-free Australia. Based in Melbourne with a chain of stores nationwide. bsl.org.au

LOST & FOUND MARKET

511 Lygon Street, Brunswick East, Victoria 3057. A 1000-squared meter space full of vintage furniture, lighting and bric-a-brac. lostandfoundmarket.com.au

MITCHELL ROAD ANTIQUE AND DESIGN CENTRE

An emporium containing over seventy different dealers within its walls, and offering every kind of vintage, industrial or retro item from Victoriana through to 20th century design. 76 Mitchell Rd, Alexandria 2015, New South Wales. mitchellroad.com.au

SALVOS STORES

The first Salvation Army recycling depots were opened in Australia in 1880 and have since developed into a multi-million dollar recycling service, including one of the largest international network of collection centers, retail stores and recycled clothing export services. salvosstores.salvos.org.au

SYDNEY ANTIQUE CENTRE

Started in the 1970s, Australia's oldest antiques center has over fifty antiques and art dealers in-house selling porcelain, clocks, rugs, clothing and furniture. Not always the cheapest place to shop, but worth checking out. sydantcent.com.au

NEW ZEALAND

ANTIQUE ALLEY

240 Dominion Road, Mt Eden, Auckland 1024. A small store crammed with all manner of collectibles, small items or furniture and antique picture frames. antiquealley.co.nz

ARKWRIGHTS

92 King Edward St, South Dunedin, Dunedin 9012. Dunedin has all manner of fabulous vintage and retro stores, including Arkwrights high-quality second-hand household furniture and homewares. arkwrightsantiquesnz.com

BOX OF BIRDS

15 George Street, Port Chalmers 9023. This tiny store in Port Chalmers is a favorite, specializing in retro and vintage clothing, magazines and collectibles. boxofbirds.kiwi.nz

FERRY ANTIQUE CENTRE

598 Ferry Road, Woolston. An antiques and collectibles co-operative with loads of treasures.

FLOTSAM AND JETSAM

84 Ponsonby Rd, Ponsonby, Auckland 1011. Online and Auckland-based with a thoughtful selection of unique antique, vintage or repurposed decorating pieces. flotsamandjetsam.co.nz

JUNK AND DISORDERLY

18 Kawana St, Northcote, Auckland 0627. A 140,000-square foot warehouse filled with furniture, stuffed animals, surfboards, clocks, lamps, silver spoons and innumerable other treasures – plus a coffee caravan. junkndisorderly.co.nz

RESENE PAINTS

New Zealand's largest privately-owned and operated paint manufacturing company, with a core ethos of being a sustainable, ethical and innovative paint company. A huge color range and top quality, low-VOC products. resene.co.nz

THE VITRINE

1A Grosvenor St, Grey Lynn, Auckland 1021. A 500sqm warehouse of original vintage industrial and antique furniture, lighting, large glass jars and other decorative items from all over Europe. inthevitrine.com

TRADE AID

Online and with stores throughout the country, Trade Aid stocks a range of quality handmade and fairtrade homewares and textiles. tradeaid.org.nz

VINTAGE WAREHOUSE

173 Ferry Rd, Phillipstown, Christchurch 8011. A treasure trove of retro and vintage collectibles.

VINTAGE WONDERLAND BOUTIQUE

179 Ferry Road, Christchurch, New Zealand 8011. A wide selection of retro homewares, tools and more. facebook.com/VintageWonderlandBoutique

Photography and Prop Credits

Cover
Front cover and author photograph Tony Brownjohn

Front pages
Page 3 photography Tony Brownjohn
Page 4 photography Tony Brownjohn

Introduction
Pages 6–7 photography Jane Ussher

The Life Cycle of Everyday Things
Pages 12–13 retro lamp from Flotsam and Jetsam,
    flotsamandjetsam.co.nz, photography Jane Ussher
Page 14 photograph of sofa Amanda Reelick
Pages 16–17 photography Jane Ussher

Your Creative Eye
Page 20 photograph of files Tony Brownjohn
Page 22 photography Tony Brownjohn
Page 23 photography Jane Ussher

The Kitchen
Page 36 photography Jane Ussher
Page 40 vintage Smiths clock from The Vitrine,
    inthevitrine.com
Page 43 photograph (bottom, right) Jane Ussher
Page 45 photography Jane Ussher
Pages 46, 47 wire caddy from flotsamandjetsam.co.nz
Pages 48, 49 photography Tony Brownjohn

Somewhere to Lounge
Pages 52–53 photography Tony Brownjohn
Page 54 photography Tobias Heeringa
Page 63 photograph (left) Tony Brownjohn
Pages 66–67 French leather armchair (circa 1950s)
    from inthevitrine.com

Bedrooms
Page 78 Jielde lamps from inthevitrine.com
Page 85 striped cushions, Lithuanian linen sheets
    from Izzy and Jean, izzyandjean.com

Space to Create
Page 88 photography Tony Brownjohn
Page 91 vintage glass battery case from
    flotsamandjetsam.co.nz, Jielde lamp from
    inthevitrine.com

Stepping Outside
Page 108 vintage French watering can (large) from
    inthevitrine.com
Page 109 photograph (top right) Jane Ussher
Page 113 photography Tony Brownjohn
Page 119 photography Jane Ussher

Lights and Mirrors
Pages 124, 125 Stranges Lane, Christchurch,
    New Zealand; Filigree Fine Jewels filigree.co.nz
Page 128 Mirrors (bottom left and right) from
    Chaos Collections, Christchurch, New Zealand
Page 130 reclaimed wood block paintings by
    Marja Broersen
Pages 132–133 Resene paints
Pages 138–139 frames from Junk and Disorderly,
    junkndisorderly.co.nz

Things to Sew
Page 146 photography Tony Brownjohn
Page 151 photography (excluding top right) Tony
    Brownjohn

Tips and Tricks
Pages 168–169 printer's materials from Junk and
    Disorderly, junkndisorderly.co.nz
Page 180 photographs of crackle chair Tony Brownjohn
Page 187 photography Tony Brownjohn

Acknowledgements

I am very grateful to New Holland publisher Christine Thomson for first suggesting that I write a book and for all the team at New Holland for their part in making *Reclaim That* a reality. Thanks to Dave Atkins, managing director of ICG for facilitating this project. Thanks also for the encouragement of all my colleagues in the *Good* magazine team and others at Tangible Media, in particular Melissa Gardi, Tracey Ellin, Jai Breitnauer, Natalie Cyra, Samantha Smith and Daryl Simonson. It is wonderful to work alongside talented individuals and I also acknowledge the valued contribution of photographers Jane Ussher, Tony Brownjohn, Amanda Reelick and former colleagues at *Good*, Rebekah White, Sally Fullam and Louise Thomson. Special thanks to Karen Warman of Resene Paints for her ongoing backing of my many and diverse projects – and for the fabulous palate of paints that I have to enjoy playing with. Also to Junk and Disorderly, The Vitrine and Flotsam and Jetsam for the use of props.

   Thanks to my extended family and friends for your interest in this book project and for your helpful feedback over the last six months, in particular my dear friends Lorna Duley and Pamela Freeman. Also to Molly Bergquist, Jade Pound and Yukari Maeda for help with photo shoots. To Gary the cat and Oscar the dog for photo bombing so many shots you both also made it into the book.

   Finally thanks and love to my marvelous husband Vincent for your unfailing support and many contributions – personal, practical and professional – as well as to my gorgeous children Levi, Tobias, Theodore and Wilhelmina who have all, at different times, carried props, acted as hand models, made me coffees or otherwise patiently put up with the disruption of yet another photo shoot in our home.